No Right Way

No Right Way
The voices of mothers of incest survivors

Tracy Orr

Scarlet Press

To my dear son, Nicolaas. May you grow up
to respect the integrity of all people.

Published in 1995 by Scarlet Press
5 Montague Road, London E8 2HN

British Library Cataloguing-in-Publication Data
A catalogue record for this book is available from the British
Library

ISBN 1 85727 087 8 pb
    1 85727 092 4 hb

Designed and produced for Scarlet Press by
Chase Production Services, Chipping Norton
Typeset from author's disk by
Stanford DTP Services, Milton Keynes
Printed in the EC by J W Arrowsmith, Bristol

Contents

Acknowledgements

I would like to express my deepest thanks to the following people who were so helpful during the process of writing this book:

To the four women who told their stories. You are wonderful and courageous women who were determined to make a difference.

To the agency where I first met the women whose stories are found in this book. Thank you for your dedication to social justice.

To Amy Rossiter for all your time and great discussions and suggestions which inspired many of the ideas in this book.

And, finally, to my partner, Rudy Gelderblom, for your constant support, time and technical help without which this book would not have been completed.

The publishers wish to thank all the sexual abuse agencies that supplied information for the resource section in the appendix. In particular we wish to thank Kendall Hunt Publishing Company for permission to reprint part of the resources section in *The Mother's Book: How to Survive the Molestation of Your Child* by Carolyn M. Byerly, 1992, and Calgary Communities Against Sexual Abuse in Canada.

Foreword

Liz Kelly, Linda Regan and Sheila Burton, the Child Abuse Studies Unit, University of North London

This book joins a small, but significant, international literature which documents the experience of women who become aware of the sexual abuse of their children by a partner. Little sympathy and much blame has been the fate of most women in this situation, and their only constant advocates have been feminist researchers and practitioners. It is feminist work which has challenged constructions of mothers in explanatory models (and the practice which followed from this) and developed innovative forms of support for women.

But for much of the last two decades the critical contribution of feminists and feminism to making sexual abuse speakable and visible has itself been silenced. This dismissal results not only in the denial of the importance of consciousness raising groups in enabling women to speak about sexual victimisation, of crisis lines and refuges in listening and believing and providing safety and support for women and girls, but also an unwillingness to remember, to learn from history.

This is not the first time sexual abuse in childhood has been publicly acknowledged. In the nineteenth century campaigns, services, speak-outs, debates in parliament and legal reform all took place and 'first wave' feminists were in the forefront of demands for change. Then as now, feminists entered into a variety of strategic alliances with child welfare organisations. But despite over thirty years of agitation, abuse of women and children within the family disappears at the turn of century, or more accurately was suppressed, only to be 're-discovered' in the 1970's.

The voices and perspectives that dominate public discourse today are those of the professional 'experts'. Absent along with feminism are the voices of survivors and those who care for them, mothers, non-abusive relatives, fosterers and adopters, and/or residential workers. Survivors are only required by the media to speak their pain, to – in the all too revealing language of journalism – make features 'sexier'. Carers are invited to tell their stories when they fit the preferred theme of insensitive and unjust agency intervention. The complex issues involved for carers in making sense of confusing knowledge/experience/information, of daring to name what is happening as abuse, of struggling with what to do and what the consequences might be of doing or not doing it are seldom addressed, let alone understood.

Accounts by individuals can provide access to the complexity and messiness of lived experience, and the stories of the four women in this book exemplify the potency of making personal histories public. A story telling methodology is used, which allows women to have more control over the process, recounting painful memories at their own pace, and place their experience within its context. But personal experience occurs within broader historical and cultural contexts, and awareness of this adds to rather than subtracts from our understanding. This foreword is intended to provide such a wider context.

Whilst the four women whose stories are presented here live in Canada, this piece draws on the issues common to most countries which have begun developing more effective responses to sexual abuse in the last two decades. Readers who wish to explore some of these issues further, and to reflect on the differences between contexts, are urged to begin with some of the sources cited at the end.

There are a number of fundamental questions which we have had to confront in acknowledging sexual abuse in childhood, these include: what is sexual abuse in childhood?; how common is it?; who commits it?; why does it happen?; how should we respond?; what are its consequences?; and how might we prevent it? The answers we give to each of these questions have implications for all the others and the questions themselves interact with one another in obvious and not so obvious ways. Not addressing each of them in a systematic way accounts in part for the confusion many of us experience, which was exemplified in Britain, but not caused by, what is now called the 'Cleveland crisis'. (Campbell, 1988) It is possible to view these questions as purely academic ones, yet they are precisely the questions the women whose stories comprise this book struggled with, some of which still preoccupy them.

On one level it ought to be fairly simple to define what sexual abuse is, on another level definitions underlie disagreements between professionals, researchers and individuals. Some definitions make any sexualised interaction between an adult, who has power and access to knowledge, and a child, which is done either for the gratification of the adult and/or which humiliates and undermines the child or young person, a form of sexual abuse. It can include touching, flashing, making sexualised comments as well as various forms of rape. Others prefer to specify types of behaviour (often excluding behaviour where there is no physical contact) – seeking certainty about the boundaries between intimacy and abuse. Still others (including many abusers) argue that there can be nonabusive sexual contact between adults and children. Too many definitions used in textbooks and quoted in procedures specify that child sexual abuse is something that adults do to children, thus excluding abuse by peers and older children. Whilst much abuse is committed by known and trusted individuals, a sizeable proportion is not. (Finkelhor, 1979, Kelly, Regan and Burton, 1991)

The confusion and lack of consensus evident in the literature is echoed in the difficulties children and their carers have in deciding whether what they know/think is happening is abuse. Children and young people lack the knowledge which would enable them to name their experience confidently, and many abusers deliberately manipulate children's perceptions. This planned confusion can take a number of forms: misrepresenting their behaviour by saying it is normal (but has to be a secret); obscuring the boundaries between affection/love/sex; suggesting that it is the child (or other people, including the child's mother) who 'makes' them behave in this way; by describing what they do in innocuous words (for example, tickling) so that others will be confused if the child does tell; and/or by limiting their behaviour to acts which are not defined as assaults, or serious assaults, in law (such as touching, sexualised talk). Children's carers seldom witness the abuse, and even if they accidentally do there may be an alternative explanation proffered. Unless their child tells them explicitly, mothers are left with a vague sense of unease and concern, bits of information, suspicions which seldom constitute indisputable 'evidence'. Even when they 'know' they often do not know in any detail precisely what has happened. As Carol Ann Hooper puts it:

> The term commonly used to describe the breaking of
> secrecy is 'discovery' – a term which suggests a single point
> in time when all is revealed. Women themselves often
> talked of 'finding out'... For some women there was a
> clearly identifiable point when they found out about the
> abuse, for others it was a cumulative process... Discovery
> is an active and interactive process which develops over time
> and has no clear beginning or end. (Hooper, 1992)

It is not only mothers who have dismissed suspicions of abuse
as 'paranoia', or who have been unable to ask the 'right' questions
at the 'right' time, or who have been unable to protect particular
children. Some or all of these are true for everyone who has child
protection responsibilities.

The answer to the question how common sexual abuse in
childhood is depends crucially on how it is defined. Researchers
may define it in relation to particular activities, and/or the age
or social relation of child/young person to the abuser. (Kelly,
Regan and Burton, 1991) The police and lawyers have to work
within the definitions currently encoded in the law. Wherever
lines are drawn more or less experiences are included/excluded.
It is this difference in definitions (along with variations in methods
of study) which accounts for the different findings in research
studies to date.

But we can say with certainty that sexual abuse in childhood
is far more common than previously thought, and depending on
the definition used between 30–70% of girls and young women
and 10–40% of boys and young men experience some form of
unwelcome sexual attention before they are 18 (based on studies
from US and UK). Sexual abuse is also distributed relatively evenly
across class and race differences. Those of us who deal with this
issue daily have this knowledge at the forefront of our minds. The
majority, however, live with a vague awareness that it is more
common, but that it is other families, other children who it
happens to. Hence beginning to ask if this is happening 'close to
home' involves questioning more than what is occurring in our
own household, it includes challenges to our perceptions of
abusers and families.

The overwhelming majority of abusers are men – yet this 'male
monopoly' is frequently obscured, especially in relation to incest
where we constantly read about 'abusing parents' or 'abusive
families'. The latest variant of this particular form of denial is the

suggestion that many more mothers sexually abuse their children, but the abuse is hidden because they have legitimate access to children's bodies. Apart from the conflation of necessary physical care of children with abuse, there is currently no empirical evidence to support this assertion. The fact that men are so massively overrepresented as abusers leads directly to profound questions about male sexuality and the structure of the family. Popularised images and representations of child abusers and rapists as 'monsters', 'evil' and 'sick' serve to hide the fact that most men who abuse children are ordinary, 'nice men'. The disjunction between popularist images and reality acts as a further barrier for children and mothers being able to name abuse and abuser.

How sexual abuse is explained represents the single most important aspect of how mothers have been responded to. When the issue returned to public prominence the dominant approach within professional practice drew on a family dysfunction or systems approach. The fact that the model only applies to incest has recently been recognised as a limitation. Drawing on Parsonian functionalism, which was in turn based on systems theory from electronics, the family is conceptualised as a system which has a surface and depth structure. To be a 'normal' functional family, the deep needs (care, warmth and sex) must be satisfied through the surface action. In a dysfunctional family this does not happen and a variety of solutions may be adopted to 'remedy' the problem – one of which is incest. Thus incest is transformed from the problem to be dealt with into a symptom of the real problem – family dysfunction.

Underpinning the theory are a set of assumptions about men and women and familial relations. Implicit throughout is the assumption that families are functional when men's needs are met, and the major responsibility for failure to meet the deep needs is allocated to women. Many feminists have noted the immense amount of explicit and implicit mother blame in this approach (Hooper, 1992; MacLeod and Saraga, 1988); mothers 'collude', or in the supposed more liberal term used by many practitioners (including some feminists) today 'fail to protect'.

We have all 'failed to protect' in so far as we have not heard what children have been trying to tell us – but it is only mothers who are targeted for culpability in theory, law and practice.

Family dysfunction theorists also persist in representing men's sexuality as driven and uncontrollable – for them it is obvious, not requiring explanation, that men seek sexual gratification with their daughters if they are dissatisfied with, or refused sexual access, to their wives. Implicit in this position is an assumption that adult women, and especially wives, are responsible for satisfying, or at the very least, controlling male sexuality.

These assumptions and the focus on the 'family system' and 'family dynamics' often result in the family as a whole being seen as the cause, and even the agent, of abuse – it is an 'abusive family'. It is the logical outcome of this perspective that children cannot be protected within such a family until all the members have been treated and returned to 'normal functioning'. The only action open to a practitioner working with this model when a child tells, or sexual abuse is diagnosed, is to remove the child.

Feminist analyses of the family highlights that it is not a community of equals but structured around two axes of power – gender and age. When linked to the recognition that men historically and currently use sexual violence as a way of asserting and maintaining control over women and children, it is possible to explain abuse inside and outside the family, and the gendered distribution of victimisation and offending. Abuse of women and children occurs not in families which have gone wrong, but which 'function' according to 'traditional family values'. To talk of rehabilitating the family in family dysfunction terms is to seek to reassert traditional sex roles and boundaries – factors which play a part in incest in the first place.

Each of the women who tell their stories in this book talks of how her sense of herself as a woman has changed, and how she thinks about women more generally, in coping with the discovery of abuse and its aftermaths. Not living with their respective partners (even if only temporarily), having to make sense of what happened, having to take new and different kinds of responsibility and decisions changes them, and changes them in ways they value. Circumstances they would not have chosen create a context in which they question many of the assumptions about women, mothering and families.

Whilst strong challenges have occurred to mother-blaming in theory and practice (Hooper, 1992), its forms are both multiple and pervasive. A common populist example was a feature article in the *Sunday Mirror* in September 1989. The headline read 'As child murder statistics soar, the *Sunday Mirror* asks: when will mothers learn?' Three 'case histories' were presented of women whose male partners had murdered one of their children. The first woman had never seen any evidence of abuse before the child was killed; the second was herself the main target of abuse and was beaten whilst trying to protect her child; the third was the mother of Maria Colwell who talked of trying to stop her husband by threatening him with a knife. Just what these women, and the rest of us reading this article were supposed to 'learn', was never specified. The only logical conclusion one could reach on the evidence presented was that since men obviously cannot be trusted, women should 'learn' to do without them. This was not the intention of the piece. Rather it drew on, and reinforced, the strong cultural message that women are responsible for what happens in families, and in the process three male murderers were not just invisible but also exonerated.

Mother blame needs to be placed in the context – as it was for each of the women in this book – of mothers being held responsible for family well being, and particularly the expectation that women, and wives especially, service men physically, emotionally and sexually. Whilst systematically denied social power, women are held responsible for men's sexuality, men's violence and children's safety.

In attempting to understand women's position we have to begin from honestly reflecting on what one's own response would be as a mother to suspecting, let alone being told by someone else, that the man you had chosen, trusted, loved had assaulted your children? Wouldn't your first response be shock, wondering if it really could be true, wishing it not to be true? The reasonable initial reaction of 'I just can't believe it' is far too often read as a statement of intention not to believe. It is all too often simply a response to what one mother has called 'the worst thing I could possibly imagine'. Add to this all the other feelings and emotions that women will experience at the point where they really begin to take the possibility seriously, and you have a woman in need of support and recognition of her pain.

Where support exists for her as a mother and as a woman she is much more likely to be able to believe and support her child, where it is absent she is more likely to believe the man's denial. The fact that she herself may also be being abused by the man, she too may be terrified of him must be taken into account. Sometimes the most effective form of child protection is woman protection.

The stories we seldom hear are those of mothers who struggle to understand their unease, their child's distress, who believe when children tell, who divorce or separate in order to protect their children. Mother's who chose their children, mother's who struggle alone and unsupported with the devastating consequences of abuse on their children, themselves, their lives. The sexual abuse of one's child changes everything: how one sees oneself; relationships with others; how one understands mothering and family; the past, present and future. As these women's stories illustrate it resonates with virtually every element in a woman's life. Abuse damages relationships between mothers and children, and as some of these stories show it can be difficult, if not impossible, to repair damage which neither mother nor child is responsible for. The powerlessness which some mothers feel in the face of this can approach despair, since nothing they do or say seems to make any difference.

In finding ways to make sense, cope and respond women draw on the resources that are available to them, and which help ease the pain. It is not surprising that the most valued resource is other women in similar situations; they understand the messiness and confusion, they know that decisions you take in good faith can have unintended consequences, they know that love and hate are not mutually exclusive, they understand that sometimes nothing you do seems to make any difference to your child's distress, they too may have searched for an explanation to the 'why did he do it' question which is livable with. It is also not surprising that in the face of the unthinkable many women turn to institutions, such as the church, which provide a framework of sorts for dealing with loss and unanswerable questions.

Women's stories provide us with clues as to what makes a difference for them, what enables them to cope despite the massive losses they face. It requires a perspective which seeks to enhance the empowerment of mothers. Which in turn must begin from a recognition of what they have done, how they have attempted to protect children, the role they play in mediating between conflicting interests, including outside agencies, and their own victimisation and survival. Women's stories make clear that what made a difference for them was being able to make sense of what was happening, having accurate information, access to understanding and support and being able to connect what has happened to themselves and their children to wider issues. Most mothers want to find ways that they can make a difference for their own children, and possibly for other children and mothers in similar situations.

The prevalence and forms of sexual abuse of children, perhaps more so than that of adult women, disturbs because it challenges fundamental beliefs and structures: it spotlights the illusion of families as safe, nurturant places; it problematises conceptions of adults as protectors of children, and since the vast majority of abusers are male and heterosexual it raises uncomfortable questions about the nature of heterosexual masculinity. Many mothers come to ask these fundamental questions in attempting to come to terms with and make sense of what has happened to their children and themselves. Yet more 'discoveries' take place, of the absence of justice, the lack of appropriate support, and the perplexing question of when, if ever, can men who have abused be trusted.

Some mothers discover that feminists are also asking these difficult questions, some find support from them and some join in the political movement against sexual violence. Others do not make these connections, but become part of this struggle in different ways. Mothers of children who have been sexually abused, like their grown up children, comprise many of our most eloquent, angry, and effective campaigners. Together feminists, mothers and adult survivors are, rightly, perceived by many as threatening – since our concern is not simply that sexual abuse is recognised and named, but with the enormous task of resisting and ending it.

1 Introduction

The study

This book sets out to explore the experiences of women whose daughters were sexually abused by their fathers or stepfathers. By sharing their experiences and feelings, these women resist the stereotypical roles a patriarchal society would have them assume. Their stories defy easy categorization and reflect the complexity of the real lives of women hurt by the sexual abuse committed by their partners. Other women whose partners have committed incest can find here support and encouragement for the difficult decisions they must make. Healthcare professionals who encounter sexual abuse in their practices may find this book helpful, as may those who regularly provide services for family members after sexual abuse has been disclosed – such as Child Welfare[1] workers, counsellors, shelter workers, social workers and psychologists.

What has been written previously about mothers of incest survivors has usually taken the form of an indictment of women for failing to protect their children or otherwise failing to fulfil their traditional roles. Stereotypes of mothers in 'incestuous families' abound and the experiences of mothers are frequently seen through the pain-filled memories of daughters, or the daughters' therapists, and are rarely first-hand accounts. This takes away the responsibility for sexual abuse from the male perpetrator in the family and instead focuses blame on the mothers of the abused children, making them the scapegoats. There is a pressing need to hear the voices of mothers of sexually abused chidren. What has been the effect of the abuse on them? What about their lives and relationships?

---

1. Child Welfare or Children's Aid or Family and Children's Services, depending on the region, are government-funded agencies in Canada legally responsible for child protection.

I am prepared to believe that there are no such creatures as 'mothers in incestuous families', nor are there typical features or traits that somehow distinguish them from other women who are oppressed under patriarchy, including me. They may have been sexually abused, have suffered from depression, work outside the home, or have a variety of interests. So have any number of women; the labels attached to these mothers, although comforting in that they try to make sense of a horrific situation, just do not fit. In the final analysis, to be a mother of a child who has been sexually abused by her father or stepfather is to have no right way to respond.

Where it all began

I once worked in my capacity as a social worker with a woman whose daughter had been sexually abused by her father. As I grew to know both the woman and her daughter, who was a teenager at the time I knew her, I was touched by their separate pain and their struggles in relationship with one another. The experience stayed with me long after I left the geographical area where they lived.

Looking more closely at the research in the area of sexual abuse, I found a lack of accounts by mothers of sexually abused daughters. I decided to focus study on their experiences as *they* saw them rather than focusing on a specific relationship such as that between mother and daughter. I asked four women, all members of a Mothers' Group[2] in southern Ontario, to participate in a research project. Before agreeing to participate, each woman reviewed a copy of the actual research proposal which was originally presented to a local sexual abuse treatment centre. After agreeing to be interviewed, the women received an additional letter of information and signed consent forms. They also received the first draft of the manuscript.

When women describe their personal lives, how they tell their stories, their words and narrative are very important and for this reason I felt that long unstructured interviews would best allow

---

2.   Refers to a support group in a local social service agency in Canada for mothers of sexually abused children.

the women's own voices to come forward.[3] This method allowed me, as Hagan (1986)[4] puts it, to: 'obtain rich and detailed descriptions of the respondent's own concerns, opinions and actions in her own words, rather than eliciting bits of behavioral responses to pre-categorized stimuli'. By listening to women's personal experiences of oppression unencumbered by the structured, pre-categorized questions and tests of the more traditional research methodology of the dominant culture, it is possible to catch a glimpse of the social relations and organization in which these women's lives are embedded.

The women participated in two interviews which each averaged one and a half to two hours in length. The first took place within a year of the disclosure of sexual abuse, the second about a year after the first interview. So that the women would feel comfortable in the interviews, I went to each woman's home to conduct them. They took place in a kitchen or living room and were usually preceded by a cup of coffee. In each case I began the interview with an invitation for Laura, Beth, Fay and June to start their stories where they wished. For most, the beginning was their daughter's disclosure of sexual abuse. There was never a problem of what question to ask next.

Each woman's story was very different from the others, and what they saw as important points also differed a great deal. My role throughout the interviews was that of active listener. I sometimes asked questions to encourage elaboration or clarification, but otherwise I listened.

The interviews were tape-recorded and transcribed. The names of persons and places were changed to maintain confidentiality and the transcripts were organized by annotating the women's words. In this way the profiles of the women in this book emerged quite naturally. Each chapter is based on portions of the woman's own words, loosely organized using my annotations and interspersed with my interpretations where I thought this important. In effect, each profile is a combination of our efforts and not necessarily a direct representation of the reality of the woman

---

3. In *The Everyday World as Problematic*, Dorothy Smith (1987) reflects on the discovery that the personal is indeed the political and says that 'this locates an oppression invading our most intimate relationships, the immediate particularities of our lives and the power relations between persons' (p. 211).

4. Hagan, 1986, p. 338. See also Bogdan and Taylor, 1975.

interviewed.[5] Afterwards I reviewed the annotations in the context of all the interviews. In this way the reader is able to hear each woman's story separately and also to see where experiences are shared by the women.

Throughout the project there were difficulties that arose out of my own ambiguous feelings and I had to struggle with my own socialization as a woman. I felt pressure to join somehow with the prevalent blaming literature about mothers or, more often, to discount it entirely and perceive the women I interviewed in the opposite light of 'the good mother'. Such polarization between either good or evil denies the complexity of the women and their lives. It is not surprising that, as a product of patriarchy, I should also have felt pressure to accept such a split view.[6]

I experienced a variety of emotions throughout the process of transcribing and writing, and I was unprepared for the intensity of feeling as I spent hours inside the women's stories. Each woman's story had a profound effect on my own emotional state. I felt almost overwhelmed as I related Fay's position of perpetually being in the middle with no right way to respond. June's story was often uncomfortable and alarming, due to the messages throughout her life experience that sexual abuse was 'normal'. I was fortunate to have the support of others, which allowed me to feel the pain and shed some tears.

My greatest fear, as I continued to write, was that I would unwittingly produce a work which would result in more anger or blame being added to that already experienced by the women in the study. Part of that fear was justified by the reaction of some of my colleagues and others who became angry upon hearing the topic of this project, let alone inquiring about its substance. Several times over the last few years I have had the experience of being silenced and being pressured by others, albeit unknowingly, to change the study to reflect more dominant views of mothers of incest survivors. In our society all of us are trained automatically to view mothers and their activities in a negative light, holding them accountable for any breakdown of the family. I wondered how I could possibly produce a work that would not be readily open to such an interpretation and felt an incredible

---

5.   Rossiter, 1986.
6.   Such splitting has been identified by Janet Sayers 'as a defense against recognizing contradictions in social relations' (Walkerdine and Lucey, 1989, p. 146).

urge to protect the women in the study. In places where I was in doubt of my own feelings, I opted for more direct quotes and less of my own interpretation.

The further I went in the writing of this book, the more I came to respect the complexity of the lives of the women I was writing about, the enormous pressures they faced and the responsibilities they have been left with. My greatest wish is that, together, we can present what actual women have experienced as mothers of incest survivors and challenge some of the myths about them perpetuated in our society.

What has been written?

In the patriarchal dream of marriage, motherhood and happy families, there is no hint of the nightmare of children assaulted by men within the family. In this dream there is no information on how to protect children from those men.[7] In our society women are taught that they should be mothers and should want to be mothers.[8] The worth of being a woman is often based on how 'successful' she is in her roles of wife and mother, and her very identity comes to revolve around these roles and relationships. Women are held entirely responsible for the well-being and raising of children, and if anything bad happens, they are to blame.

There has been very little research which even attempts to address the unique experience of mothers of female incest survivors. Literature and research abound with references to the mother's part in causing sexual abuse to occur by failing in her roles as wife and mother. In fact, mother-blaming runs rampant throughout major clinical journals. Two authors, Caplan and Hall-McCorquodale, published a review of 125 journal articles detailing a total of 72 kinds of psycho-pathology in children seen as caused by their mothers.[9] The occurrence of sexual abuse is frequently attributed to mothers, who are seen to collude in the sexual abuse of their daughters or to abandon them in all sorts of ways. Mothers of female incest survivors have been described as narcissistic, ill, physically or emotionally unavailable, or otherwise unable to

---

7. Driver and Droisen, 1989.
8. Caplan, 1985.
9. Caplan and Hall-McCorquodale, 1983.

protect their children.[10] I can only cringe at the hostility in some of the literature (particularly the work of Suzanne Sgroi and family therapy literature) so often aimed at the mothers of sexually abused children and at the attention that seems to be so quickly shifted away from the perpetrators of the abuse.

Judith Herman (1981) challenges the myth of the 'collusive mother' and three prevalent stereotypes of mothers: first, that she 'failed to perform her marital duties; second, she, not the father, forced the daughter to take her rightful place; and third, she knew about, tolerated, or in some cases actively enjoyed the incest' (p. 42). Herman makes an interesting connection between professional groups which encourage these stereotypes of women and pornographers.

Sexual dysfunction

In their review of current family therapy literature, James and MacKinnon (1990) describe the many references to mothers of incest survivors as 'frigid', ambivalent about their sexuality, unable to tolerate intimacy and depriving their husbands of sexual contact. Suzanne Sgroi (1982) talks about a prevalence of sexual dysfunction in such marriages, reinforcing the myth that the sexual abuse of children is an act of sexual need or the failure of women to meet men's sexual desires. Men's sexual needs, regardless of frequency of intercourse, are seen as normal, while women's sexuality is deemed dysfunctional. This interpretation of male functioning and needs as the norm occurs without examination in much of the literature on sexual abuse. O'Hare and Taylor (1983) challenge this stereotype, stating that research does not show the occurrence of such a condition as sexual dysfunction is greater in families where incest occurs than it is in 'normal' families. That men have sexual intercourse with their wives while they also assault their daughters is rarely mentioned.

Distance

Women are often described as distancing themselves from their families, thereby allowing sexual assault to occur. Writers such as Sandra Butler (1978), Herman (1981) and Michell (1988) have reviewed the most common profiles or stereotypes used to describe mothers of incest survivors. Butler (1978, 1985) has critiqued

---

10. Koch and Jarvis, 1987; Michell, 1988; Renvoize, 1982.

theorists' definition of 'desertion', which includes mothers working outside of the home, having outside interests, having another child, and having emotional problems or physical illness/challenges that prevent them from taking on their expected roles as wives and mothers (p. 113). She points out that women who look after their own needs, such as following up interests or pursuing a job or schooling, are seen as having abandoned their families. Herman (1981) also calls attention to this sexist double standard which prevails in family therapy literature, where it is only women who are labelled by authors as abandoning children through work or disability.

Sgroi's (1982) *Handbook of Clinical Intervention in Child Sexual Abuse* is probably one of the most highly regarded and most frequently read books in the field of child welfare in Canada. In many ways it is an excellent reference, but in describing mothers of incest survivors Sgroi resorts to many myths and stereotypes, including the belief that:

> the women often tended to be psychologically absent in their relationships with both their husband and their children. They seemed to exhibit a lack of psychological investment in the interpersonal aspect of their marriages and family lives ... one should note that the wives chose and, to a certain extent, 'set up' their responses and modes of interaction. Psychological absence is an excellent defense mechanism and at the same time an effective method of escaping responsibility. (p. 193)

By emotionally withdrawing from their daughters and sexually depriving their husbands, mothers are sometimes seen to set the stage for incest or abuse to occur.[11]

Systems theory

Almost all of the literature I have reviewed either sets out stereotypes for women who are mothers of incest survivors,[12] or critiques these stereotypes.[13] Family therapy literature often places mothers

---

11. James and MacKinnon's (1990) review of family therapy literature.
12. Koch and Jarvis, 1987; O'Hare and Taylor, 1983; Renvoize, 1982; Sgroi, 1982.
13. Butler, 1978, 1985; Caplan and Hall-McCorquodale, 1983; Driver and Droisen, 1989; Herman and Hirschman, 1981; James and MacKinnon, 1990.

within what has been termed the 'incest' or 'incestuous family'.[14] James and MacKinnon (1990) provide a review of family therapy literature and a critique of its myths about the 'incestuous family'. Indeed, the term 'incestuous family' implies a broad responsibility for the abuse. By failing to take the patriarchal context of abusive behaviour into consideration, family systems theory shifts responsibility and blame away from the perpetrators and on to both mothers and daughters.

Object relations theory has also been used to blame mothers. Koch and Jarvis (1987) state that although actual sexual contact is the responsibility of the perpetrator, the mother's symbiotic relationship with the daughter and her subsequent narcissism create an atmosphere for incest to occur. The mother's role is seen as central. Michell (1988), on the other hand, sees the social organization of gender and patterns of male psychological development as producing narcissistic *men* rather than women who are more likely to parent in ways that treat their children as extensions of themselves. In *Incest: A Family Pattern*, Renvoize (1982) supports the view of a mutual 'agreement' among all family members to maintain secrecy and avoid separations, as well as the mother's 'unconscious collusion' in and denial of the abuse.

Systems theory describes incest as a way the family uses to defend itself against separation and loss. Such an explanation implies that fear of separation and loss *causes* incest and that *all* family members conspire together in the assault on the daughter to avoid loss.[15] I support O'Hare and Taylor (1983) when they make the point that inappropriate family dynamics where incest is occurring may be an *effect* of incest, not the *cause*. Systems theorists cite a lack of involvement of family members outside the home, so that incest maintains the rigid boundaries of the 'incestuous family' where there is too much interconnectedness or enmeshment within the family nexus. There appears to be either too little connection, and therefore abandonment, as in mothers distancing themselves from their families, or too much connection, resulting in enmeshment within the family nexus. Once again the responsibility of men for the assault of children, and the societal context of patriarchy which supports it, are lost and both mothers and children are blamed.

---

14. Koch and Jarvis, 1987; O'Hare and Taylor, 1983; Renvoize, 1982.
15. James and MacKinnon, 1990.

Societal context

Some feminist literature referring to mothers of incest survivors tends to retain stereotypes but adds a societal context. Butler (1978, 1985) brings in the concept of cultural oppression and emotional isolation when she writes about mothers of incest survivors. This starts to bring the occurrence of incest out of a damaging family systems perspective. She uses excerpts of interviews with women who are mothers of children who have been sexually abused. Butler reviews some of the profiles of mothers as infantile and dependent, victims of sexual abuse themselves, sexually naive or sexually dysfunctional, and applies a different analysis. She provides potential reasons why women fit these profiles in a world where women are oppressed, while also calling attention to the prevailing lack of analysis of why a man would make his own child a 'sexual surrogate' (p. 115).

While Butler clearly connects these mothers with the oppression of all women and refutes any connection that would remove responsibility from the abuser, her analysis tends to retain some of the more familiar stereotypes. In her second edition of *Conspiracy of Silence*, under the heading 'The Problem Reconsidered', she refers to the great variety of male offenders and the dangers of woman-blaming, which offers offenders a range of excuses (p. 211). But it is also likely that women who are mothers of incest victims may vary as widely as the victims or perpetrators themselves in terms of socio-economic status, occupation, race, religion, sexual, physical and mental health, and family history. Perhaps the very categories into which women who are mothers of incest victims are placed need to be questioned and dismantled, rather than explained in different terms. In this way we may begin to understand their lives in all of their complexity.

James and MacKinnon (1990) have noted 'patriarchy to be the pervasive and overarching context in which we are psychologically and behaviourally constructed' (p. 87). They have also pointed out that some feminist accounts of incest do not provide an analysis of patriarchy, so that incest becomes interpreted as the power of individual men over women and children.

To date there has been little written that focuses exclusively on the life experiences of mothers of incest or sexual abuse survivors. Most information, such as that found in Judith Herman's (1981) *Father–Daughter Incest*, comes through the painful memories and expressions of adult daughters. The actual voices of the mothers have not been heard. It is the voices of these women that I have attempted to record in the chapters which follow.

2 Laura

Laura is a woman in her late 40s. At the time of our first interview she had been married for 26 years. She has three children: Benjamin, who was then nearly 20; Susan, just 19; and Jeff, then ten years old. Laura's husband, Tom, sexually abused their daughter from the time she was four years old until she was 13.

Susan disclosed the abuse to a counsellor at the age of 18. Laura did not begin to suspect sexual abuse until shortly before the disclosure, and did not realize that her husband was the abuser until after her daughter disclosed the abuse to her counsellor. She immediately found a safe place for Susan and made the difficult decision not to allow her husband back into the home until her daughter should agree to it.

At our first interview, four months after the disclosure, the family's form is drastically altered and Laura has difficulty coping with it. She has few supports: a Mothers' Group and a single close family member. She anticipates blame from both friends and professionals and is reluctant to confide in anyone. She has failed, in the eyes of a patriarchal society, to be empathetic and understanding to her children and husband; blame from society at large and from professionals is not long in coming.

Much of the interview with Laura highlights her struggle to make sense of her relationship with her husband and her relationship with her daughter. Throughout the interview she is able to repeat that her husband was responsible for the abuse and that her daughter was in no way responsible. She is unable, however, to focus the resulting anger solely at him and cannot help redirecting some of it at Tom's parents, herself and her daughter.

Laura felt her husband and daughter had a good relationship. She knew symptoms of sexual abuse and never noted any in Susan. She never suspected sexual abuse until an incident one evening. Tom had made some cutting remark to Susan and her daughter withdrew to her room very upset.

It was on a Sunday night. So I went up to her room, she was sitting on the bed just rocking back and forth and crying and I went in and put my arms around her and said, 'You know honey, that remark he made was uncalled for and I will talk to Daddy to make him understand your feelings,' etc., etc., and she kept saying, 'He hates me,' and she was – not hysterical, but she was very upset and crying and what have you.

We had been like that for about ten minutes, with me just hugging her and rocking her and letting her vent her frustrations because I felt they were legitimate. She was not over-reacting. She was hurt and this was how she was expressing it. Anyway, he came to the door, stood in the doorway just for a couple of minutes, and then he made some comment to her about he was sorry and she said, 'Yeah, yeah, yeah, you're never sorry,' and she turned and looked at him when she said that and there was such a look of hate in her eyes. I don't know, I've tried to recall [the actual words] for you but I can't. There was some phrasing there, the way she was reacting.

Anyway, at this point my husband said something about, 'Susan, you're over-reacting to a simple situation.' He said, 'I think you need help, have you ever considered coun-selling?' And she said, 'Yes I have,' and he said, 'Well, I really think you should. Do you want to make the appointment? Should we leave this in your hands or do you want Mom or I to make the appointment?' And she said, 'Mom can do it.' Well, my husband did it, the next day, which surprised me but I understand this often happens. Like, he was trying to get help to her so that she could control her feelings before a disclosure was ever made ...

There was something in that conversation that kind of clicked in my head and I can't remember the exact wording, but anyway, when we came down it was about 10:30. My husband and I sat in the living room and I said to him, 'You know, I can't help feeling, the way she is reacting, that she has been sexually abused somehow.' And there was an instant look of fear that crossed his face and then it vanished and he was saying, 'Oh, come on! Now you're over-reacting.' And I was saying, 'No, I just can't help it. It's a funny gut feeling that I have,' and that was about the only conversation we had about it then. But, you know, every day it would sort of flit through my mind: 'Who could it possibly be?'

Once Laura suspected that her daughter had been sexually abused, she made a mental tally of all the close males with whom Susan had contact in an attempt to identify the perpetrator. She ruled out friends, feeling she knew them well enough to know whether they were capable of abuse. Her two brothers? Not likely. Her own dad?

My father's been dead six years but naturally you think, 'My father?' No, never! My father was the most wonderful person in the world.

Tom's dad?

She [Susan] had very little to do with Tom's father and he's been dead for five years, so it couldn't have been him. So you're going through all the male relations and I couldn't imagine it being any one of them. And I never once thought of my husband.

The actual disclosure was first made to the counsellor whom Susan saw after the incident described above. Laura found out about the sexual abuse from Susan after she came home from a session with the counsellor and relayed her counsellor's suggestion she move out of the house.

And I said, 'I'm finding that very unusual, Susan, what's the reason?' I was very puzzled and I can be very [persistent], I keep pushing, pushing, pushing. And I said, 'OK, P [the counsellor] feels you should move out of the house. Are we looking at a long-term project here or short-term?' 'No, I think we're looking at a long-term.' 'OK, do you ever see yourself moving back into the house?' And then she said, 'No.'

I just knew that I was on the right track, with my gut feeling. She has an older brother, Ben, who will be 20 in October. There's no way that I could ever see it being Benjamin, our son. And, I don't know, there was a lot more to it. But anyway, I finally said: 'Susan, I can't, I don't know how to say this to you, but the only thing I can possibly think is that you have been sexually abused by your father.' And at this, you could just watch her face start to disintegrate and crumble and she paced around the kitchen and the tears were flowing and she said, 'How did you know? You were never to know. You were never to find out.'

Tom would be home in an hour. Susan was frightened and, naturally, did not want to be home when Laura confronted her husband. Laura acted immediately and found a safe place for Susan with some of Susan's friends, promising not to tell her Dad her whereabouts. She then went to see Tom's sister and brother-in-law, Janet and Ted.

[They] were [among] our best friends. And I went to them and received a lot of support. I didn't know who else to turn to. I mean, my whole life was in tatters at that point. And I knew I would have to confront my husband that night but, you know, how? Anyway, I stayed with Janet and Ted until 9:30 and decided [what to do]. Ted said, 'Do you want me to come with you, are you fearful or anything else?' And I said, 'No, I can handle it.'

The decision to confront Tom was the most difficult for Laura.

You'd be surprised. That's a big issue. Because you realize that by confronting him you are then taking the steps to alter your entire life.

As of the day of the disclosure both Susan and Tom left the house. It is implicit in Laura's description of the steps she took after the disclosure that she took responsibility for what would happen to the family. This was a given. Laura is in the middle, trying to salvage the family, including her daughter and her husband whom she still loves.

As I say, I see the positive steps for her trying to rebuild. As to where my husband and I go, I've thought a great deal about that. I do love him, part of me I guess. I miss him but I will not give up my daughter for him. Needless to say, I wish I didn't have to make that decision ...

And I guess what makes it so difficult is the fact that she is basically gone from my life anyway and my husband should be in it. But because of the abuse and her feelings on it, my own feelings on it, but [especially] her feelings on it, he has to stay out of the house.

Her decision not to allow her husband back into the home until her daughter agrees to it causes Laura a lot of pain and loneliness, but it is the option which is most likely to keep the family intact. Any other

choice would result in the loss of either her daughter or her husband,
which is unacceptable to Laura. The change is difficult for her, with
family members living separately in different parts of the city as well
as the strain of trying to maintain some type of communication with
one another. Laura feels she cannot confide in even her closest friends.

We talked about people's attitudes earlier about abuse and
the attitude towards the wife. That has been one of the main
reasons why I have not disclosed to any of the girls that I
work with or any of my friends, even my best friend,
because I'm afraid that they will think that a lot of the blame
is mine. 'What's the matter with her that he had to turn
to a little kid?'

Laura fears that professionals will blame her as well, even though she
has a good sense of who is ultimately responsible for the sexual abuse
of her daughter.

So anyway, I've been putting off counselling. I also keep
putting it off because I don't know whether I want to get
into all this crap. It's hard work going through counselling.
And I keep thinking, OK, I know I've got problems but the
situation that I'm in I don't think [is because of] my
problems as such. OK, I'm not a perfect human being.
Everybody can improve in a certain way, but this situation
is not my fault. And I don't know if emotionally I want to
get into all the hard work and I'm afraid of getting a
counsellor who will be judgemental.

Laura is angry about the abuse and badly hurt, 'devastated' even, and
she cannot possibly rationalize her husband's conduct. Nevertheless,
she feels she ought to be understanding. Haven't abusers been abused
themselves?

They [abusers] have very low self-concepts, it really is not
a sexual issue, it's an issue of control. I keep thinking I should
be more understanding, I realize this is an illness, I'm not
to take it personally, it's not against me, it's him – you know,
this type of thing. But it still does [get to me]. It's not just
that he's been unfaithful to you, he has been unfaithful to
you with the last person in the world he should.

Laura also attempts to understand her husband by reflecting on his family of origin. He is a product of inadequate parents who, she feels, are responsible for the way Tom turned out as an adult.

> He grew up an abused child of an alcoholic father, a martyr-syndrome mother. I think they should never have had kids, either one of them. Even if they had each married somebody else the kids would've been the ones to suffer – and then you put the two of them together raising five children. Those kids all have had such monumental problems. I always figured my husband was the sanest of the lot, [but] it made for a very difficult marriage because he has no male model to follow as far as being a husband is concerned. He had no idea what a father was. He had no idea of how to express love. He wanted to but he had nothing, no personal knowledge, on which to fall back. It caused a lot of problems.

This argument relieves Tom of some of the blame and helps Laura feel sympathetic towards him and to maintain her relationship with him.

Some anger surfaces when Laura talks about her and her daughter after the disclosure. She is clearly not blaming Susan for the abuse and realizes the horrible effects the abuse has had on her: she has had to move out of the home, there has been a suicide attempt, her marks at school have dropped, and plans for university and travel have been put on hold. Laura is supportive of her daughter in all practical ways, but at the same time she feels Susan is lacking in understanding for her predicament.

> What she was doing was pushing me to make an ultimatum, like: 'It's either me or Dad, you can't have both. You will not talk to him, you will not associate with him.' And I tried to explain that to her, and I never once questioned her when she told me. I simply hugged her, said I believed her. But I said, 'Susan, you've got to understand, we have a joint business, we have a house that's owned jointly, we have two other children besides you that know nothing of what's going on. Your father's out of the house, but I must communicate with him, I must see him and he has a right to see his other kids.'
>
> You know, she was very upset by that. We went through a lot of tears, etc., etc., but I felt, at this point, she was manipulating me. And I felt that I had to let her know that,

although I could appreciate what she was going through, I also had decisions to make that affected my life. I'm not just going to walk away from a house, jeopardize my other children's future, because I'm madder than hell at my husband.

Also Susan has the time and opportunity to heal, she has her adult life before her. Laura's prospects of rebuilding her life, she feels, are much poorer than Susan's and the chances of rebuilding a relationship with Tom are in part at Susan's mercy.

[Tom] also realizes that he will not come back into our lives unless Susan allows it. And that's basically [impossible] until Susan has healed to the point where she confronts her father and they can talk maturely and honestly. And maybe they'll never be friends again, I don't know. I'm not going to give up my daughter. And yet in a lot of respects you're really torn there because, as I say, she's 19. She's at the age where she would be getting out of the house normally anyway. She was talking about going to [university], so she would be out of the house and only home for holidays or whenever she chose, and I mean, that would probably not be very often because, knowing her, it would be a full social life outside university.

We're now on the point where she's getting to be an adult and she would come home only when she wanted to. And I guess that what makes it so difficult is the fact that she is basically gone from my life anyway and my husband should be in it. But because of the abuse and her feelings on it, he has to stay out of the house.

Laura is ambivalent about her relationship with Tom. Her anger at him begins to surface, and then fades as she starts to consider the future of their relationship, its possible loss and the cost of keeping it.

I could take it better if he went to bed with his own mother, you know what I mean? I don't know who would want to, but I mean it. I get so angry at him to think, 'How could he wreck her life!' You know, his own daughter.

At times it is possible to put away the reality of the sexual abuse by quite consciously pretending for a while that the disclosure never occurred.

You know, when my husband comes here, I can forget about it. We had already bought the airline tickets and Jeff was involved, our ten-year-old who was coming with us. We were to go to Los Angeles for a week. So we went to Los Angeles and my husband had already booked it anyway. When we travel with the kids we always take a suite. And so I took the one bedroom, Jeff took the other bedroom and my husband took the couch. So there was no sex. I feel nothing sexual for my husband at all. And yet we still have kinda fun together. What we agreed to do was to pretend and, anyway, we took Jeff with us, and I must say in a lot of respects I had a good time.

Laura is thankful that Tom is still in the relationship. Her usual role in their relationship can no longer be fulfilled now that he is not in the home.

I am amazed that he is willing to stay married while he works out his problems, you know what I mean? Like to accept the situation and continue paying the bills and, in essence, not getting anything for it. Like he's not getting the comfort of house and home. He's having to do his own laundry unless he can bring it over here and say, 'Do you have any loads of whites that have to be done?' You know, he's not getting any of the emotional support he used to get.

Laura's relationship with her daughter has also changed, of course.

I wouldn't say [prior to the disclosure] we were ultra-close, but I think that for a lot of important decisions for her, she would at least tell you about things if not ask your advice. It was perhaps, 'I decided, you know, to do such and such, or this is what I want to do.' Occasionally she would say, 'What do you think of such and such?' I guess that's what astounded me so much, because oftentimes these were not just discussions between she and I, it was between my husband and I and her where we would sit down and talk about what she wanted to do musically with her life and those type of things. As I say, I guess we seemed to have such a good family relationship, but it really, really kind of bowled me over in that way.

After the disclosure Laura found that her role as mother had been effectively usurped by the counsellor. It is she who assisted Susan with plans for her life and goals while Laura watched from a place outside. Laura's relationship with Susan became more distant, and even her role in sharing her daughter's plans or acting as a sounding board was removed.

> I have to admire the kid in many ways, because there have been times when she hasn't had a cent. When I could I gave her money; I tried to give her $350 a month to pay for food, you know. The friend [she was staying with] didn't ask for any money for rent. It was a young couple she was staying with. What she did was clean their house, what have you, and occasionally go out and buy groceries and things like that. But anyway, P set this all up. I was wondering how on earth can I get money to her, etc. on a regular basis. P applied for student welfare and suggested that she quit her job because she would be too torn between too many things. I can't necessarily say I approve of it, but anyway, that's what her counsellor says and I have no right to interfere. So Susan has quit her job and is in this apartment and I guess will be receiving student welfare. When she was over last Sunday for supper she didn't have hardly anything in the house. I think she had two eggs and what have you and I said will you please go through the pantry, the fridge, etc., and she left here with two bags. So that's fine, you know. And it hurts me.

Laura accepts the counsellor's role with her daughter and her authority. When Tom suggested writing Susan a letter to apologize, she directed him to talk to Susan's counsellor, who would know her daughter's needs better than she would. She also wanted to protect her daughter from further pain.

> It may make him feel better, but what's it going to do to her? The second thing [he said] was that he should go to the police and report himself. He's thinking of those things and I said, 'Before you do anything would you please talk to your own counsellor, would you talk to P as to how it will affect Susan?' I don't want her to go ahead and have more guilt thrust upon her, when she's only started to face reality. There's just so blinkin' much to it. I don't know if he's saying that just to get a reaction out of me.

What does Laura wish for her family now?

Well I guess it's like everything, there's reality and then there's, 'Gee I wish.' You know? Like your ultimate wish is that hey, your husband gets a better understanding of himself and gets to heal his problems because he's obviously got a lot. My daughter gets to heal her problems and somewhere down the road they can face each other. Perhaps with the understanding that he had a problem which gave her a severe problem but would make her more empathetic and understanding of what his problem was? And perhaps [we'll] never be a family unit as such again, but then families are constantly changing anyway and the whole essence of it is the children leave home and everything. That changes, so I guess that's the ultimate wish. That's the dream. If you get it, terrific; if not, we'll deal with what we got.

Women are denied legitimate outlets for, or direct expression of, their anger. Anger focused on male perpetrators who are also husbands may result in loss of support for one's self and one's children. Laura has learned that to be a good wife and mother, to be female, means to be empathetic and understanding of men. She may wish her daughter to develop these same abilities. Difficulty arises when the man is Tom and he has sexually abused their own daughter. Laura's interview shows above all a woman and mother whose anger at an unbelievable act has been expressed in the only way remotely acceptable in our society: away from the male responsible and on to the women around, including herself and her daughter.

The second meeting

A noticeable change had taken place in Laura when I met with her a year later. She has come to recognize how her feelings had been dismissed and submerged. She is now determined that she will feel whatever way she feels and will not allow that to change. Her relationship with her daughter has improved, while that with her husband continues to oscillate between love and anger and distrust.

The relationship with her husband has been an ongoing challenge. Reaching a satisfactory relationship with him is a long-term project; Tom himself has come to share this view. Laura sees his controlling behaviour as the biggest obstacle in the way of a good relationship. Most of the time she talks about Tom's controlling behaviour as clearly his responsibility. She will not accept the view that she could have prevented the abuse by being a 'better' wife and mother; however, she cannot absolve herself completely. Sometimes she frames Tom's behaviour as a relationship problem, a problem which she, as a part of the couple, will attempt to address in couple therapy with B. Perhaps better communication between Tom and herself could have prevented the sexual abuse. For a moment then, her view of Tom's responsibility for various abusive behaviours, including sexually abusing his daughter, is clouded.

Over the past year Laura's process of recovery has articulated what behaviours from her husband she will and will not accept and she respects her own feelings. No longer will anyone dictate what she is to feel. Even depression is legitimate and part of her recovery. She has survived the last year with all of its conflicts and disorganization; whatever life has in store for her, this year has shown Laura that she will be able to manage whatever comes her way.

Laura describes what the year has been like for her as the blackest period of her life.

> And yet it has been the most productive. In some respects when you look at it, you think at the time it's the longest year of your life, and yet in a lot of respects it's the shortest. But it's the most conflicting.

Her relationship with her husband is a major source of conflict. He is still living outside the home and she has, as yet, not decided what she would like to do about the relationship. She has seen changes in her husband, but she is aware a closer relationship with Tom might compromise her own needs. Tom is attempting to find help through various services and, just as before, Laura is appreciative of his efforts in counselling.

> He's trying very hard to change and it's very evident. His whole way of approaching things has changed slightly to moderately. He still has a long way to go, which he realizes, but he is still in private counselling and realizes he will be for quite a while. He goes to Alanon, to Adult Children of Alcoholics, once a week and feels that that's probably the most beneficial ...
>
> From the time of the disclosure, B first took him for a month until he got him a private counsellor. Tom went to Offenders' Group but really didn't find that quite beneficial. He found that the majority of the men there were still not accepting responsibility. They were still laying blame on the wife and on the victim, on society, this type of thing.

And he felt that this wasn't helping him at all, to listen to these people signing in about how abused they themselves were and misunderstood and all this. So he quit Offenders' and in place of that he found Alanon to be extremely helpful.

Laura and Tom have also attempted to find services that would address their problems as a couple.

Couple's [therapy] through an agency is the only thing like that in the community for offenders and wives and it was not being helpful to us at all. We were meeting every two weeks, which is far too long. It should be a weekly session, especially when you first start off.

We understood that you were to learn how to communicate better, how to express your emotions, relate things more clearly, how to learn to rebuild trust, how to talk about the offence, the abuse and all the problems that went around it. You do this in a group setting with other couples who have been where you are now and they do most of the guiding. Neither one of us is perfect and they would say [things] to both of [you] at one time and challenge you, try to make you see things from a different perspective perhaps, or tell you not to come on so strong. But nothing ever developed. The other problem was, we often had our meetings cancelled and when we did meet we weren't doing anything. And we're spending so much time out of the house and still [have] kids that [need us]. We felt that it was a waste of time. So we are starting joint counselling with Tom's counsellor and we will see how it goes. Our first appointment is [coming up]. That may not work. If not, we'll simply go for something else. But I think I can work with [B]. I just don't know if he has done very much of this couple's counselling. He has done a lot of offenders' counselling, so we'll just have to throw it all together.

Overcoming the negative lessons learned as children is difficult and requires hard work, work to which Tom appears committed. But Laura feels she has a great deal of healing yet to do and will not consent to his moving back into the house.

He really wants to. He wants very much to be back in the house, but he is quite willing to accept whatever my decision

is. Right now I still don't know. I'm trying to find out
what my feelings are towards him.

She has identified the biggest problem her husband has to overcome.

You see, aside from the sexual abuse of my daughter, my
husband is or was a very controlling man, very manipulative, very controlling of finances, emotions, sex, everything.
He would tell me how I was supposed to feel about
something. 'You can't feel that way, you shouldn't feel that
way.' And when I first started in therapy it was, 'Why
aren't you healing as fast as me? Why aren't you understanding this problem as quick as I am?'

*Tom has a tendency to measure her recovery in his terms, relative to
his progress.*

Until we finally got talking about the issue of control;
that's, I think, probably going to be the main hurdle that
we have to work out with B. He can't tell me, he can't make
me heal, he can't make me feel something.

*Tom's controlling behaviour has been acted out in many ways in his
relationship with Laura and the rest of the family up to the present
time.*

He was very moody before and his moods would control
my life. The kids and I would sit there, you're playing with
the kids when they're small and you know he's due home
from the office in five or ten minutes and you feel this knot
growing in your stomach. What's his mood going to be
when he walks through the door? Now if he opens the door
and says, 'Hi honey, I'm home!', then the knot disappears.
But if he comes in and you hear the door slam and grumble,
grumble, grumble, the knot just gets tighter. But you see,
if I ever mentioned that to him, how I reacted when I
found he was moody, he would shift the blame back to me:
'Well that's your problem if you can't deal with it', 'I have
no problem with it, why on earth should you get a knot
in your stomach?' This type of thing. Everything was always
put back on me; I was always being put down.

Laura's process of recovery over the last year has made that clear.

Yeah. At least there's time now to say, 'I won't put up with that.' ...

And he understands now, or is starting to understand, exactly how much control he exercised over me and the children and how he manipulated, how he controlled. And I think it will help with him being aware of it and trying to change that. Hopefully, we can be two equal people in marriage.

Has Tom's counselling helped with that? Does this issue come up in his counselling?

No. That actually hasn't come up in his counselling. That has just been he and I talking, but, as I said to him, I don't want to go into it too deeply, issue by issue, until we have an impartial third person there. But I don't even think that his counsellor realizes how controlling he has been. You see, he can only acknowledge and treat him for what Tom wants to share with him.

So unless it's made explicit ...

That's right. It doesn't get talked about and is not perceived as a problem and yet to me that is one of the greatest problems. His control emotionally would be to deny my feelings, negating my thoughts, so you start [believing it]. Like if you're told often enough that you're stupid, you're going to eventually believe it. I think that's what happens with a lot of kids. And the same thing happens in a marriage. I mean, if somebody keeps whittling away at you, you eventually start to lose confidence in being able to perceive this marriage the way it really is and compare it with other marriages. I also am not in the mood to believe that all marriages are good. We show people what we want them to see and then we close the front door. The whole thing can be different.

Laura will no longer put up with control over her feelings and has realized the profound effect her lack of freedom has had on her.

And actually I realize, I have realized for years, it sort of turned into a self-hatred. I can't punish him, I punish myself because I feel I compromised too much on important issues. He's had nine affairs that I know of. Some were two-

or three-night stands, one lasted two years. Sporadic, but still.

That must have hurt.

Yes. Well, you see, I only confronted him once and this was after [the affair ended]. You know when your husband's having an affair, but you say it's not really happening. So you use this denial bit, because if you do confront him you realize that your whole life has changed. You now have to start making decisions. 'Do I leave him? How do I support the children? Am I,' the old Ann Landers'[1] question, 'Am I better with him or without him? Are the children better with him or without him?' So I made compromises and stayed in the relationship. We went to counselling for a year, our marriage definitely improved then, but he never handled the issues of his control.

Like many women, Laura has taken on the socially prescribed roles of wife and mother, but she now views her roles in the family differently and she rejects the idea that being a 'better' wife would have prevented the abuse:

There's no such thing as supermom, superwife. Having a clean house did not prevent my husband from abusing my daughter or running around on me. You know, putting nutritious, delicious meals on the table every day didn't prevent that. It is communication …

He had to go through the experience of disclosure, being told to leave the house, in order to seek counselling. If there had not been the crisis, we still would be going on in a rather superficial marriage where I was resentful of his control and he was controlling and I couldn't make him understand it and never trusting him because [of] his affairs. I was never allowed to talk about them. 'I said I'm sorry and I don't want to deal with it again.' How's that for control? 'I'm sorry if I hurt you, but just bear that pain.' End of conversation. 'I said I'm sorry. What more do you expect?'

So in that way we are starting to communicate. He is really opening [up to] a lot of those things. So we'll see where we go. If we make it, terrific. If we don't, I probably still could

---

1.   Ann Landers writes a popular advice column that appears in many North American newspapers.

be his best friend. I don't think I would, but I think I'm being generous when I say that.

She is now determined that she will feel whatever way she feels and will not allow that to change.

Her views about men in general are changing. There are and have been some really positive men in Laura's life.

Oh, for months and months after the disclosure, I lumped all men in with my husband. I became a great cynic. Thought the male race absolutely stank and if they all fell off the face of the earth I wouldn't be one bit sorry. I've come to temper that a great deal. I look at my own two sons, I look at my two brothers, their father that was absolutely terrific and I realized that you can't be judging all men by my husband. I'm a lot more fortunate than most people because I do have a lot of positive people in my life and some of them are men. So they can't be all bad.

In the past year Laura has watched both her daughter and her son develop relationships. She is pleased that Susan's boyfriend, Geoff, treats her well and that he has fitted into the family. Susan has told her boyfriend about the abuse and from what Laura can see they have a playful relationship, unlike the more sombre and serious relationship she had before meeting Geoff. It is gratifying for Laura to see.

Oh, it's fantastic. To see her in a relationship where she has trusted the person. I asked her what Geoff's reaction was when she told him about the sexual abuse and she said that he comforted her and said, 'But the sad part, Susan, is that this is all too common and it's kept so well hidden.'

Laura also likes Benjamin's girlfriend, Jennifer, and how his relationship with his girlfriend has developed. She is both pretty and intelligent and she and Benjamin have been the best of friends for 14 or 16 months.

Well, about six weeks ago Ben came and he said, 'Can I bounce a few ideas off you?' It was the fact that he was beginning to realize that he cared much more deeply for Jennifer than just a best friend, that he was fearful of changing that relationship because once you go from friend to girlfriend and then things don't work out, you've lost not only a girlfriend, you've lost a friend and he was fearful of losing her as a friend. And so we talked about it and I

simply responded that that's something you and Jennifer
have to decide together. And so he said yesterday, 'Mom,
we made it official last night. Jennifer and I are going
together.' Which is great. It doesn't really change anything.
She's over here most of the time anyway, but she's a real
nice person. So if things work out for them as they get older,
that's great, but it's a good relationship. But it surprises me
his maturity in, 'Can I bounce a few ideas off you?' Just not
kind of rushing into it. So I can say I'm very pleased with
all my kids.

*In talking about both her son's and her daughter's relationships, she
focuses on mutual respect and the ability to share feelings as well as
to trust and nurture: qualities which have not often been present for
Laura in her own relationship with her husband.*

I think men often feel smothered when it's the women
always doing the nurturing. Like I think men enjoy that
nurturing but then it bounces back, they feel guilty for
accepting it. You know: 'I should be more manly or
shouldn't need this.' They ask for something and then
they feel resentful when they get it because other emotions
come into play.

*Laura's relationship with her husband continues to oscillate between
love and anger and distrust. They talk a lot more, he is more gentle
and doesn't take her for granted any more, she may fall in love again
if he keeps it up – but there is still the distrust, and what about respect?*

Perhaps I've taken a few fledgling, baby footsteps [towards
conciliation], but – no. In the background there is still a
lot of distrust. And that's what I don't know. If that cannot
change, you cannot build a relationship without trust.
And you see, another thing, I lost a great deal of respect
for my husband. With each affair that he had, I lost respect
for him, but with this child abuse, I lost absolutely all
respect for him and I don't know whether I can build that
up again. So I will just have to see.

*Her relationships with her children, like that with her husband, have
become more open over the year. She appreciates them and finds oppor-
tunities to tell them so.*

I don't let a day go by without telling my kids, directly or
indirectly, that I love them, that they're important to me

and I [have] found that they respond in kind. Jeff at least says it every day. Benjamin oftentimes doesn't say 'I love you.' He'll say, 'Gee, you're terrific.' He always manages to say something positive. And even Susan, as I say, not an evening goes by that isn't opened and closed with a big hug, a kiss, and 'I love you, you're terrific.' You know, that type of thing. So it's changed my perspective of mothering. I find [more and more] the most important thing is to heck with the dirty room, to heck with the, 'You don't pick up your socks or your glasses or your dishes,' what have you. So what? In a few more years my kids will all be gone.

The boys have been supportive and caring and this has been great for Laura. Ben takes on a lot of chores he would not have considered before; the lawn is mowed, the walk is shovelled and occasionally supper is made. Laura appreciates the break she gets when these kind of things happen.

Laura has also seen an improvement in her relationship with her daughter. It seems to have shifted from a superficial relationship, seen by Laura as controlled in some ways by both Susan and her counsellor, to a more open relationship where most subjects and feelings are allowed by both Susan and her mother.

I can remember one day, it was just before Valentine's Day because we had to stop and get milk and there were those little cinnamon hearts on the shelves, and as I was driving her home she said that there were times, many times, that she wished she had never disclosed to me. And she asked if I ever felt that way and I said, 'Yes, there have been times when I've felt that way, but when I really analyse it, I'm so very sorry you were abused but I am never sorry that you disclosed. We have a much better, open relationship and oftentimes we talk more like friends than the old mother/daughter.'

They discussed the possibility of Susan moving home again.

She feels that she is now too old emotionally to move back home, that she would find it difficult to be held accountable to somebody for her comings and goings, to have to be here at specific times for mealtimes. To continue to be herself, be the little messy thing that she is and know how much it irritated me would bother her. And as we explored our feelings, we both felt that it would be probably mutually beneficial to both of us if she continued to lead her own little life, in her own little apartment and come home whenever she wanted to. So that's basically [it]. I see her probably no more often than I did before, at least once a week, maybe twice a week, but it's a much easier atmosphere entirely, especially considering what we went through.

Laura sees a lot of progress in her daughter's growth. Susan is now a woman instead of the girl who had to leave home.

She, I think, had very short teenage years because I think [for] a lot of her teenage years she was still a little girl – I think because of the sexual abuse and never dealing with it. So she stayed at that little girl stage even though her body said, you're well into your teenage years. And then I think with the disclosure, that was her teenage years and they were painful and she very quickly blossomed into womanhood in this past year. And I think that's where she [has mellowed]. I don't know whether her change is permanent because I really don't understand much about this Movement. I certainly hope it is [permanent], but we'll wait and see.

During the year Susan joined a group called 'the Movement', with which Laura also has become involved. Prior to joining the group, Susan had been involved in individual counselling, which didn't seem to help her very much. As Susan tells it, the counsellor was always challenging and questioning her feelings, insisting that really she felt something different from what she was saying.

And P was forever telling her that she had to sue my husband to heal herself, which caused a lot of problems between Susan and I because I felt that at the present time her motives weren't right and that she might harm herself and her brothers more by going public. She still had four years to lay a criminal charge and she had the rest of her life to lay a civil charge – or vice versa, I don't know. So anyway, she found this Movement through somebody at high school and it has made a great change in her life.

The basic philosophy at the Movement is that you look at the world today, our globe, and you see violence, hunger and starvation, mistreatment of people, and recognize things that you don't like. You can't do anything as an individual person about such things as starvation in Ethiopia or civil wars, various strife. But perhaps by looking at yourself and getting to know yourself you can change something within your own house, or on your block, among the people you work or play with. By understanding yourself better and by approaching people differently, you may stop one little act of violence. Start doing things in a small way and then you get more and more people involved in the Movement.

Laura credits this group with providing a service which has helped Susan in her recovery.

So I found it interesting because, as I say, coming back [from a meeting] with Susan she said she bore her father no malice, she didn't hate him and I said, 'I'm very pleased for you, but,' I said, 'I still hate him.' And she said, 'That's because you have not gone through the releasing revenge part.'

Susan apparently accomplished 'releasing revenge' through a combination of mental imagery and desensitization where she faced her greatest fear, which was meeting her father on the street, and practised relaxation and guided imagery until she could face it without fear. But Laura questions to what extent Susan has in fact put her suffering behind her and whether she really has come to bear her father no malice or ill will.

I keep thinking, 'OK, she's setting him up.' That we'll go to this family wedding where there will be all of my relatives and in front of this crowd of 250 people she will announce that she has been sexually abused by her father. So I'm not really going to have a comfortable time there until, I guess, we're driving home again.

In her reassessment of her relationships with others and her views of herself, Laura also found herself dealing with images of God, reassessing her faith and spirituality. For fear of having to explain the absence of her husband, she stopped going to her friendly, small church community and she grew cynical of her church's version of God.

I think God is much greater than what Christians make [Him] out to be. I think God is not only Christ: I think he is Mohammed, I think he is the God of everyone's religion. As I say, He is, to me, omnipotent. And I think He is much more charitable and loving than Christians make Him out to be. They [talk about] so much guilt and so much hellfire and brimstone. I think God is much more understanding of our problems and our psyche, why we make the mistakes that we make and that type of thing. I think He's much more just; I hope He is, anyway. I've made some stupid mistakes too. But I think that, when I look around just at the beauty of this backyard, of the world, when I look up at the magnitude of the universe, to me there has to be a supreme being to orchestrate all of that.

I think man has made God really narrow. There again, we live in patriarchy. Control, and how else to control but by definite rules and regulations. Poor God, I think He's blamed for a lot. If it isn't God, it's the Devil.

As Laura rereads her diaries, she finds very positive memories of her father. He was an environmentalist before it was popular to be one and a very gentle man. She cannot remember him ever hitting her. He would yell at her sometimes if she upset him, but he would sit down and explain why not to do something. It is the kind of image she likes to have of God.

Laura now works part-time as a nurse but feels she could go back to work full time one day and make a comfortable living.

I could probably make twice as much money as I could in any other profession, especially now with the latest contract they negotiated, because they would start me minimum at the five-year level [of seniority]. I wouldn't be living in luxury but I certainly would not be starving. And, as I say, I have other skills I could certainly look at. And my husband still continues to pay all the bills, oftentimes throwing in a little extra.

She has evidently planned her own and her family's recovery.

Yeah I have. I've had to because even trying to decide where I want to go with my husband, you have to look into the future and see far down the road. I'm basically at times very lazy: 'Do I want to go through all this hard work?' And it is hard work. You know, it's very emotionally draining. Also it's not nice to have to look inside yourself. It's scary, to have to put definite labels on your thoughts, your feelings, to have to pull them out and look at them from all angles, and then they go back inside. So you're constantly examining everything. But once you start it you find out that it's not as scary. As I say, I had suppressed everything for so long that it was such a relief finally to bring it out. It was such a relief to feel depressed.

For Laura to be able to feel depressed was a part of her recovery.

Yeah. To be able to sit down and say, 'I feel depressed today.' Well, that's OK. I'm entitled to that depression. So I'm depressed now. Maybe I won't be depressed in a half hour, maybe I will be, it's immaterial. It's how I feel. With luck I won't be depressed for long, but [it's good] just to acknowledge your emotions without having to feel guilty or to justify them or what have you. It's simply me. OK? Here I am and I can accept that, so it's a great day. I feel wonderful. Isn't that fantastic?

It was a relief for her not to have to smile all the time.

Oh, you get trained like a puppy, so you could be raging mad inside and someone would knock at the door and you'd open it up and there'd have to be a smile, you know? And you'd keep up that facade until they walked back out the door. So I gradually adopted this style. Also I was taught at home, by my parents, that what took place in the home stayed in the home and I basically taught my kids that as well. And perhaps in some respects that's wrong, that may have led to Susan not disclosing earlier.

Six or eight months ago Laura could hardly conceive of her own and her family's recovery.

When did I start to change? It was gradual. Oh, I would say at least eight months had elapsed before I finally started to recognize my feelings and that was just a little at a time, and as you make each discovery it makes you more anxious to find out more and more about yourself.

And she is excited about her feelings. What is she going to feel like today? She has found confidence and strength in her feelings.

You could throw anything at me. It's not to say I won't cry over it. I think every parent's greatest fear is that they'll lose one of their children. But I would survive and I would be able to handle the pain of the loss. I don't want to; I hope I'm never tested.

I asked Laura if there was anything else about her own process of recovery that she would like others to know about.

Well, I think my confidence for one has changed. I think that's the biggest thing. I'm not afraid of the future. If Tom and I don't get back together, I know that I will simply go back to school, upgrade my skills.

Laura feels she is ready to live her life with or without her husband. She has survived the last year with all of its conflicts and disorganization. Whatever life has in store for her, this year has shown Laura that she will be able to manage whatever comes her way.

3 Beth

Beth is in her early 40s and has been married twice. At the time of our first interview she was living apart from her second husband and with two of her three children. She has a son, John, then aged 23, and two daughters: Lee, 21 and Brittany, 17 years old. Lee lives with her young son and the father of her son. Beth's first husband was a very violent man and an alcoholic. Beth's second husband, Conrad, was not physically abusive to Beth but he is an alcoholic. Conrad sexually abused both of his stepdaughters.

Beth first learned of the sexual abuse of her daughters six years ago when the girls told a relative what had been happening. Beth confronted her husband and it was decided then that Conrad would remain in the home. She recalls both girls begging her to let him stay. In the interview Beth was confident that the abuse stopped at that point, but in retrospect is not sure her decision was the right one. The abuse remained a secret, Conrad joined Alcoholics Anonymous and Beth supported him by becoming active in Alanon. The sexual abuse of Lee and Brittany became public when Brittany disclosed the abuse to a school counsellor approximately a year before the first interview. Family and Children's Services was called.

The most striking thing about Beth is her need to keep the family together at any cost and her fear about the possible dissolution of the family. The public disclosure of the abuse was a serious threat, and Beth felt her world was crumbling and that she would lose both her family and her self. She cannot recall a lot of the last year, which she describes as like walking in a haze. There was panic and uncertainty.

> The panic that strikes you when you don't have anybody
> to talk to is really scary to begin with. And, aside from
> Children's Aid, the girls really didn't have anybody either.
> Like, Children's Aid's one thing, but it's a methodical thing
> that you have to go through to get to the end and whatever:
> it's not a 'Sit down, let's discuss this' and feeling type

thing. Although I'm sure they do that, but it's a lot more cut and dried, a paperwork kind of thing.

When Family and Children's Services got involved, Conrad and the two girls went to meet with them. Beth was not invited. Conrad didn't even want the elder daughter to come. Beth insisted, reasoning that Brittany would need the moral support. Beth stayed at home wondering what would happen next.

I remember, you know, when they left, walking around here crying, just walking through the house wondering, 'What do I do? My whole life's in shreds here. It's all falling apart. How are we gonna ever get this together? What are we gonna do?'

Six years ago, when the abuse first came to light, she had felt it her duty as a woman and mother to keep the family together. Rather than going public with it she had preferred to 'keep it in the family' and try to work it out among themselves. Now, with the public disclosure, this decision to have Conrad stay in the home could come back to haunt her.

I have a great respect for authority, but it's always with an iron fist. So I always figure, you're gonna get caught if you don't do it right. There's no two ways about it. So I had feelings of [them] taking Brittany away from me, because she was under age and I hadn't really done what I should have done six years ago. I could see them putting Conrad in jail and going through all that nonsense. I really was afraid when they left that any of those things could have happened, you know. And I wasn't involved and I just [didn't] know what to do.

Beth stayed home and awaited judgement and possible punishment. It was easier to blame herself than Conrad.
  Being a wife and the mother of a family had been the source of Beth's self-esteem and sense of self. With the future of the family uncertain and the power significantly to affect that future in the hands of others, she didn't know who she was any more.

I didn't have a clue who I was. I was lost, just totally, totally lost. Body and mind just totally separate. I started going for counselling and I went to assertiveness training last year. I guess that was my first step. We were in a classroom out at the YWCA and there was a Raggedy Anne

[doll] on the wall and her body was over here, and her head was over there – you know, like completely apart – and that's exactly how I felt. As soon as I looked at that I thought: 'God that's me! What am I doing up there?' But that's exactly how I felt, just totally disjointed. Nothing fit[ted] together at all. So it's taken a long time to get them back in line here.

The relationship with her husband had not been good for her self-esteem either. It had been deteriorating since the disclosure six years ago.

He was pushing me further and further away; and as the rejection grew, I got smaller and smaller and smaller and smaller until I just felt like I was an absolute nothing, and I can see it in my mind 'cause that's exactly how I felt. I'd be lying in bed at night and I'd just be aching for him to put his arms around me and [I'd] just reach over and touch him and he would actually cringe and move away from my hand. Those feelings of utter rejection absolutely tore me apart and I just felt, like I say, I could just see myself getting smaller and smaller and less and less until I wasn't even a being any more. I just was a shell walking around doing whatever had to be done.

Beth tries to be understanding of Conrad's behaviour in terms of his problems with alcohol, his family of origin and his current efforts in counselling. She uses what she has learned about alcoholism, a medical frame of reference, to help her understand the abuse of her children and relates her husband's recovery from alcohol to his 'recovery' from being a sexual abuser. She is clear, however, that alcohol did not cause the abuse. What relationship does she see, then, between alcohol and the abuse?

I think in the beginning we just blamed the alcohol. I don't do that any more obviously because alcohol's only a symptom, it wasn't the problem at all. The problem was much deeper than that. Alcohol's not the problem, it was a cover-up.

But it [the alcohol] contributed to the set of circumstances [surrounding the abuse] at the time, and I believed that I [could] live with that situation, but I certainly couldn't live with the situation at all if he wasn't getting the help personally, [the help] that he needs for the other problem of abuse. Like he was abused as a child when you go back,

way back when – all those things that led up to that, which
I don't understand. But then I don't understand why I'm
the person I am today either.

Are his recovery from alcoholism and his recovery from sexual abuse
similar? Beth has concerns. Conrad has a daughter, Jayne, and four
young grandchildren. Might he abuse them?

He's in a stage of his recovery that [it] would be really a
stupid thing to do and he's not capable of doing it at this
point, but I want a 100 percent guarantee that it will never
happen again. But see, I don't have a 100 percent guarantee
that he'll never drink again, so without that I can't say that
he won't abuse again either, given the right set of circumstances, because that type of recovery is not 100 percent.

Conrad was getting counselling and Beth's and Conrad's relationship
was changing, but progress was happening so slowly that Beth couldn't
be certain they would ever get to the end. At some point she just
couldn't afford to wait any longer and, to Conrad's chagrin, after the
public disclosure the two of them separated at Beth's request. There were
some things he would have to do for himself.

I have to give him credit for what he's done. I mean, he's
come a long, long way in a couple years. He's got a lot to
do himself, 'cause he still feels inadequate. That's his
problem and one that he has to live with. He has to learn
that, I can't help him with that.

She needs time for herself and her own healing.
    After the public disclosure Beth took several months off work to deal
with the stress and work on her own recovery. She was already involved
with Alanon, was having counselling and attending a Mothers' Group.

I guess everything that I do, I have to go back to the
beginning and come forward. That's how I'm recovering,
so that's how it's easiest for me to do. I, for some reason,
can't start at the end and go back. I do what I have to do
at this point, but in order to get any satisfaction for myself
I have to go back to the beginning.

So she reflects on her own upbringing. She has gone to great lengths to
keep her family together and it was like that when she was growing up
as well. There were ten children in her family, both parents drank heavily
and at least one of her sisters was sexually abused by a brother. But

everything appeared just fine to the outside world. Beth moved out of the family home with that attitude. She didn't tell her parents about the problems she was having.

> My Mom and my Dad don't know any of my problems, never did, and I lived in the same town. When I ran away [from the first abusive husband], I never told them. They didn't know about the beatings and the fights. They didn't know anything. They sort of lived in their little shell, went to work and did whatever, pillars of the community and nobody ever, ever knew.

She feels she shares that attitude with her sisters. Several of her sisters left home and got married early and each have their own problems in their families, but unknown to the outside world and unknown to their parents. Beth feels she has dealt with all that.

> I dealt with all that stuff from way back when. It took me a long time to do it. I don't feel that they have to know about it, because, I mean, my Dad's 77 and my Mom's 72 and they think they raised the most fantastic family in the world and that everybody's just super and can handle anything. So no point in disillusioning them. But Dad was just so proud when he was down [for a family reunion], he's just so proud of every one of us, you know. But he's never been able to say it, and as long as he could ignore all the things that we were going through and it didn't involve him, he could still keep us in that little shiny light. I guess, like I say, if nothing else, I know where I come from.

She had learned her lesson well as a child. When Conrad's abuse of the children was disclosed, the important thing to Beth was for the family to stick together and keep it to themselves.

> Today I believe that the reason things weren't dealt with at the time was because, for us, the time just wasn't right. I don't know whether we could have survived it at that time. Now we're surviving. Now we're going through this, we all are at a stage where we can deal with it and it hasn't totally wrecked our lives. I don't know whether [we could have] back then, had it been disclosed then.
>
> That's a cop-out and I know it's a cop-out. But I can't go back and change that, I really can't, and I truly believe that things happen for whatever reason they happen today. Like,

I am right where I am supposed to be today. So however I
got here is irrelevant. It's just, I wish that they [the girls]
didn't have to suffer as they suffered during that time, but
I don't know if they wouldn't have suffered more had we
done whatever was supposed to have been done or should
have been done back then, or if the girls would have
survived it. They weren't very strong at that time. They had
nothing to be strong about all their whole lives. They had
been holding on by thin threads to whatever was being given
to them.

You know, my life certainly wasn't uncomplicated. From
one abusive marriage into another one; my kids really
never had anything to hold on to or whatever. So maybe
they wouldn't have been strong enough at that time to deal
with the problems that would have [arisen]. Now, at least
for us, we are where we're supposed to be at. As long as the
girls can get the help now, that's important.

There was a time that Beth blamed her younger daughter for the abuse.

I don't know how that got switched around to being her
fault. I just don't know how we managed to put the blame
on her. Somehow or another it just happened. Well, it sort
of was over the years. And that's four years she was in
school. Like, that was after the disclosure and I guess I
thought it should've all been better then or something. I
blamed her for it, not me; I don't know. Maybe I thought
when she told me and it stopped, everything was going to
be OK. But as it was, she just got worse and worse and worse
and worse. I guess because we hadn't dealt with it. I mean
she didn't want to [deal with the abuse] but she did want
to, you know?

*When Beth talks about blame, she sees only two options for allocating
responsibility. She no longer blames her daughter; at present she sees
the abuse and the decision not to go public as her responsibility. She
still works to keep the family together and has managed to maintain
good relations with her daughters. She entertains the possibility of rec-
onciling with Conrad and seeks her daughters' approval for this.*

Brittany's fine. I've asked Brittany what she [would think]
if Conrad and I got back together and she said, 'Oh, that's
fine.' But Brittany says, 'Oh, that's fine' to everything.
She's just a big, easy-going, loving, whatever.

Lee is more sceptical.

> 'Well, I sure hope not,' [said Lee]. And I said, 'What do you
> mean by that?' And she said, 'After all the lectures you've
> given me and all the times you've told me, you're going
> to go and do it again?' And I said, 'No, that's not the way
> it is, Lee.' I said, 'I'm not going to rush into anything.
> We're just going to see each other again and we're just going
> to take the time and do it. It doesn't mean we'll be together,
> it doesn't mean we won't either. We might some day.' So,
> 'Oh, OK. Just as long as you're sure and you take it easy,'
> she says.

*Beth makes use of her personal history to explain why she didn't make
the 'right' response and, again, takes the responsibility and blame for
the abuse.*

> But I think I was just ripe. Like all the other things in your
> life, like I was just ripe for all the things that [befell] me.
> And when I go back and look at my childhood and all those
> things that happened there and in my first marriage, you
> know I'm not really surprised that I was blind in the second
> one. Really not surprised at all.

Considering the way she grew up?

> Yeah, and where I come from and where I've been. It
> doesn't really surprise me when I look at it, it scares me that
> people can do that but I'm sure I'm not the only one that
> has done it. I'm just lucky enough that I'm going to recover.
> I'm not at all the person I was before, I'm just not. You don't
> get to walk over me. I'll move aside, but you do not get to
> walk over me. That's that.

She talks about what it's been like to start taking care of herself.

> I am [taking care of myself] and that's really important. And
> that's really selfish, which I think you have to be. There's
> a lot of things I have to give back and I will in my own time.
> The programmes that I've been in, both the counselling and
> the group for mothers, have just been a Godsend to me –
> the same with Alanon. And although I'm taking at the
> moment, when I'm well and comfortable with it, I will give
> it back.

And Beth has been successful. She is taking things one day at a time and does the best she can to look after herself. When she does that she finds it takes no effort at all to do her best for someone else. She likes the feeling and she has learned she cannot do without her self-care, a valuable lesson to learn.

You're darned right. I bet you any money, I can't tell you a time that I felt as good. Just incredible. I have my bad days like everybody else, I get a headache like I've got one right now. But as far as feeling at peace with myself and just comfortable with what I do and say and feel, I got no problems with that any more. My life isn't a bunch of secrets any more, I don't have to hide it from anyone. I certainly don't spread this around, but I do have people that I can totally confide in. I have never felt so free. Not at all. There isn't anything that I have to, you know, keep a secret or hush up from my family or friends.

Clearly Beth has spent a lot of time in the last year reclaiming the good things about herself.

Oh, I have. I spent a lot of time. I can't believe that I've spent this much time. I've never spent this much time in my whole life on me, let alone in one given time. I've given myself a lot of months, but I can't believe how far I've come and I can't believe – I'll have to tell you – I'm really vain, but I can't believe that God made me go through all those things and got me here today so He can snuff me out tomorrow. So I think I'm going to stick around for awhile. So there!

She takes down several pictures from the mantelpiece and proudly describes the people in them: her parents, brothers and sisters, her own children and, of course, her new grandson.

The one thing I find is that we're a family again and we're total family and that's the really nice part. We're just as comfortable as this. My girls call me up, you know, like Lee calls me up to tell me these little things. She makes me so proud and feel so good. You would never know that we had been through this and still have so much to go through.

The second meeting

In some ways our second interview picked up where the first one left off. A year earlier Beth had expressed concern about the safety of her husband's grandchildren and the necessity of eventually telling his daughter of the sexual abuse of Beth's girls. This final hurdle had been overcome, but not in quite the way Beth had hoped.

> My husband finally told his daughter, probably about three weeks ago, although he told me a week ago Friday that he had a talk with her two or three weeks ahead of time, but he didn't tell me when he went to tell her. So three weeks had passed and he was in the bank and he just happened to mention [it] and I said, 'Well why wouldn't you tell me?' Like I had said I wanted him [to tell her], but also had said that I would like to be around for her in that case.

Beth thought about it for a few days and then on the weekend she called Jayne. Her son-in-law answered the phone, but after calling to Jayne he came back and told her Jayne couldn't speak to her right then.

> She's never done that before, I mean never, so I know she won't speak to me. So my husband had said, when he was telling me that he told her, 'She's very, very angry.' And I said, 'Well, I expect her to be very angry, you know.' And he said, 'Yeah, but it's not like you think.' And he said, 'Well, she didn't think she should have to know.' So however he's presented this, it's come from the other side, you see.

Conrad's daughter has been told of the abuse, but Beth has had no part in the form the revelation has taken and what anger the daughter feels has become focused on Beth and away from Conrad. In order to protect her four granddaughters, Beth may have lost her relationship with them and their mother. Beth experiences again the feeling of loss of control over a situation which she feels to be very much her business and which is important to her recovery.

> So I've spent the last week and a half trying to write, [but] I can't, I'm so upset, I can't handle the rejection at all. I can't. I have a terrible, terrible time with it. And so I was going to call back, but if she won't speak to me again, it would just do me right in. So I thought about it for a while and then I came to the conclusion that I would write and give her the choice.

She had been up till after midnight composing the letter and had actually just mailed it the day we spoke. She hadn't slept well for a few nights because it had been preying on her mind.

> So I decided once I got it out of here and put it on paper then there's nothing I can do about it, it's gone and it's finished. Whatever will be will be. But if she doesn't come around, then she won't let me have the kids in August. She's got four girls and they're the ones I'm worried about. My other daughter has a son, but she's fully aware since she's one of the victims. I just hope and pray that she [Jayne] will come to some sort of understanding in her life. You know, [it was] for her good and for the good of the kids that I insisted it be done. I didn't say a lot in the letter, 'cause I would really like to speak to her personally. I just hope she knows I'm there for her now and that she gives me a call.

In discussing their experience, Beth and her daughters realized that Conrad had things turned around. He, the abuser, had become the victim and they, the injured parties, found their pain minimized.

> Lee said, 'It's amazing how all of a sudden he became the victim, you know? He's got it switched around so we don't exist.' And I was thinking too when she was saying that. The funny part about that is that we've allowed that to happen. We did this. None of us have treated him any differently from day one. We all sort of thought that he was having a rough time and we all supported him through it.

Beth and her daughters accept a great deal of responsibility for producing Conrad as victim. Abusing the children was seen as Conrad's responsibility, what happened after that was taken on by Beth and her children. A more dangerous extension of this acceptance of responsibility for 'allowing' Conrad's behaviour after the disclosure would be to take responsibility for the actual abuse. Beth and her daughters stop short of this extreme. The concepts learned through Beth's association with Alcoholics Anonymous and Alanon, such as enabling and co-dependence, are taken up by her and used to understand Conrad as victim.

> It's the same difference as living with an alcoholic and taking on all that responsibility. You don't let them take on responsibility themselves and they're never going to get the help. And it's the same with this, you know. We sort of gave

him free rein here and took the responsibility – not guilt and shame, because I'm sure he had some of that as far as counselling was concerned, but we never gave him the chance to show it with us. Like, we didn't get angry at him, we didn't neglect him, we didn't anything. We made this as comfortable as possible for him and we made it too comfortable.

Beth and her daughters protected and took care of Conrad as they had always done, ever since the first disclosure.

And I still don't understand why, I don't have any idea why, it really annoys me why we still do it but I do it! So I can hardly blame my kids for doing it. They have a good teacher.

It just happens. And then I sit back and think, 'Why did it happen?' But I know why: because we allowed it, you know? And this situation's no different than the other. We've minimized it so much that he's minimized it. Even though it's very, very important; very, very real. He's been in counselling for two years, he's been sober for seven years – which is a lifetime to anybody that's never been around AA, doesn't know how easy it is to go back to drinking. It doesn't matter how long you're sober. Most of the people in the programme, [even after] 20 years, all it takes is one drink. It doesn't take much. But to Jayne that would just seem like forever, so why bother?

Insisting on the disclosure of Conrad's abuse to his daughter has made Beth face the possibility of relationships with family members dissolving. It has been difficult for Beth and her female children to give up their socially prescribed roles of nurturer and caretaker even in the face of abuse.

And I knew, I'd sort of prepared myself anyway. I knew once I'd made this decision that whatever the consequences were, I would have to deal with it. So whether I see them again or not is really irrelevant, no matter how much I love them and how much I want to. You know, I have to respect their right for privacy to deal with this however they have to deal with this. Because we certainly don't all deal with it the same way ...

It's entirely up to [Jayne] which way she intends to go in. If I never see them again, I have to deal with that, but it's a whole new set, a whole new game here. And if she does manage to call me and we do manage to get some sort of rapport, that would be fantastic, but it doesn't come without its problems as well. We'll just have to deal with it when it comes.

In retrospect Beth thinks she would have liked to have had the chance to tell Jayne herself. She could have been there and seen her reaction and given her comfort.

I just want to get it finished. He seems to think that it's directly against him, and it's not. It was just for the protection of the kids. These kids I've been around since before they were born. So they're just as much my grandchildren as anyone's. Whether they are legally or not doesn't matter. It was necessary for her to know, and I think she'll come to that realization sometime.

It may never happen again. I said in the letter, even the slightest chance, and there's always a chance, is just one chance too many. Kids' lives are concerned.

Beth gives Conrad credit for his efforts in counselling and AA, but she has misgivings about what changes have taken place and what remains the same. Did his counsellor help him prepare to tell his daughter of the abuse?

I was not impressed with her at all. It's not a healthy relationship and for a counsellor I was really disappointed with her at the suggestions she made. Like writing Lee a letter saying 'Do not open unless your father goes back drinking.' I mean, that's a stupid thing, why would anybody [do it]? Number one, I could never give her a letter like that. Number two, who would ever take a letter like that and not read it? It doesn't make any sense. She [the counsellor] thought I could give them another two years [before telling his daughter about the abuse], which was two more years out of my life that I wasn't about to give him. No. I've already given him eleven. That was enough.

You know, I do respect the fact that he went for help, that he's working on it. And he's really trying. I've got to give him that. And he has been sober for over seven years. And he works a programme of some sort. I don't have to agree with the programme he works, but he is working a programme and I respect the fact that he is changing his

life, however he does it. So I think you gain an understanding
and respect for people who [make] the changes that they
can make.

*Beth still hoped something would change after Conrad began counselling,
but it appeared to be just more of the same. He didn't have time to do
things because he had to go to counselling. And there was now somebody
else to tell him what to do. He still didn't have to make his own
decisions. Beth fears the time when Conrad is back on his own. She
feels that without someone confronting him with his behaviour and
beliefs, Conrad may fall into old patterns. He may seek control over
someone else again.*

Every time he has to make a decision, he has to wait. He
can't give you an answer. He has to wait and go and get
an answer and bring it back. It's two years and most people
don't go to counselling that long. Even his counsellor says
he's probably the longest client that she's had. She must
have some sort of hold on him, she's not weaning him off.
She's not letting him stand on his own two feet. In other
words, she's taken over where we all left off. But she's
taking responsibility away from him. Making decisions for
him. And that's what scares me, I think.

*Through Alcoholics Anonymous, Beth has learned to understand
Conrad in a way which separates people from their behaviour.*

I always supported him through this whole thing. I've
never ever hated him. I've been mad at me. But I definitely
did hate what he did. [I learned to] separate the man from
the act, which is easier probably because I learned to do
that in AA. I learned to separate the man from the bottle,
so in that concept it was a lot easier for me.

*But she has come to see Conrad sometimes as a stranger and does not
recognize him as someone she was once in a relationship with. She asks
herself how she ever could have been married to him; she cannot find
anything in common with him.*

That's a real shock to the system. I look at that man and
he could be a stranger ... He's somebody I met on the
street. There's just no way we have anything in common.
He doesn't think like I do. He doesn't agree with anything
I do. He doesn't like anything I do. He doesn't like me at
this point.

The thought makes her laugh.

   After the disclosure Beth saw Conrad suddenly become old, almost overnight. Their relationship seemed to have ended then.

> We didn't have sex any more. We didn't have a life together any more. And it was all at the same time when the disclosure came about and he didn't feel comfortable in the situation any more because I knew. It was OK up until the time that I knew. And once I knew, he didn't feel he had any rights as a husband, so from then on our whole focus was getting Conrad well. He became the whole focus of everything we did. We never went out socially. AA was the whole thing. We had, like I say, no sex, no relationship, no real affection. No showing of anything. Just became a totally, totally different husband.

In a way it frightened her. One day everything was fine between them because she didn't know about the abuse. Well, they had their ups and downs, but they kissed and made up.

> And then as soon as I found out, the world just changed and we were no more. There was no we, no us, no nothing.
>
>   And all because I knew. And I think what really upset me the most, is how [abusers] think. That it's perfectly all right as long as nobody knew. And he still says that today. And I've asked him a hundred times: 'That doesn't make sense to me, how can it make sense to you?'

She is really pleased, however, with the way her relationship with her daughters is shaping up.

> [Brittany] got accepted in college this fall, so she starts in January. We're so excited. Lee didn't get accepted this year, she was late getting in but she's going back to school to upgrade again. She has Jamie and Jamie's in daycare, so she has to be careful otherwise she loses her daycare spot for him, so she's going back to school and just upgrading. They've assured her that she'll get in the next semester because out of the last 45 [applicants] they only had three spots and three on the waiting list and she was the third on the waiting list and her marks are super, but they wouldn't be able to tell her until September. Being on Mother's Allowance with a little one, she couldn't wait to make that decision, because she would have had to go to

summer school, which she is doing anyway, but [she] also had to take a night course in order to catch her one credit. So she's just going to wait until next year. But they're both doing wonderful. I just sit back and I can't believe how far they've come and how lucky we are. You know, everybody survives this and it's not the end of the world. It can be dealt with.

And the one good thing about this – something good always comes from something bad – Lee, Brittany and I are closer now than we've ever, ever been. There isn't anything that we can't tell each other. We share and that kind of stuff.

Did her relationship with her daughters change right away?

No, not right away probably. It took a while because they were very angry. Brittany particularly was very, very angry with me for a long time and I don't blame her for that. She was the fall guy. So she had every right to be angry. And she's just turned that right around. She's wonderful. So she's going into social services, I think I told you, which is really excellent. But her marks are in the 80s and 90s, she's just fantastic. And Lee, she got a special award for her [work term], she's been nominated for a scholarship. She's done really well.

Beth is proud of her daughters and how they have managed their lives, but she also acknowledges that the sexual abuse of the girls will continue to affect their lives.

I can almost guarantee that at some other point in their life they'll have to get help again. Because I don't think it ever ends. I think that as much as we've all felt pretty comfortable with the situation right now, eventually something will come up down the line [which will raise the issue again]. I mean they're only young – 17, 22 – lifetimes away from reality still, you know. Lots of times before they get settled in their lives they'll have to deal with this [effects of the abuse] on an ongoing basis.

She feels that because they dealt with it successfully and in their own way this time, her daughters will be able to make their own decisions when it comes up again. Nobody is going to tell them how to feel; they will decide for themselves.

I'm just so proud of them, extremely proud. Considering that they've been through years and years of hell, not just with Conrad but with their Dad before that, the violence. Even at their ages they've suffered just about every type of abuse there is to suffer when you stop to look at all of that. Physical, mental, emotional and sexual. I mean, where else do you go from there?

Beth has learned suffering is very much a part of life. It has come to her children as a result of abuse, and to other loved ones through physical illness. She has friends currently suffering with and dying of cancer. Others have already died. One friend in particular comes to mind.

She's putting up a really good front. She's playing ball again and she's going to bicycle. She's out looking for a job and she's doing well. But she takes life as [it comes]. To watch her, the strength she has, it's just unreal. Like, it's just a part of life.

All my friends have been sick. Most of my friends have cancer or have had [it], and most of them are going to die and thank God I can handle that. You know, there must be a reason that I'm here to do that, there must be a reason that somebody's there to hold on, to hold hands. And so I take that as my calling. I take that as being what I can do. And one day someone will be there for me when my time comes. That's all I can hope and that's all I ever ask for. That somewhere down the line, whatever you give out, you get back. So, those things are still to come. And I can deal with them when they do come. And they're inevitable parts of life. But again, I have a very, very deep faith and I believe that those things happen for whatever reason they do and I have no control over them. But I can be a source of comfort in the meantime.

Beth's recovery has included much self-discovery through her involvement with nature and new people, as well as a renewed sense of her own spirituality. Growing up, when she had the opportunity, she didn't enjoy the outdoors, but now she does. She has a friend 'up north' with a farm and she went up there for a week.

It was great. I planted a garden, I planted 150 trees, made a rail fence. You know, worked all week. Worked hard for a whole week. It was great! It was really good. I have part of the garden up there now. There are three of us that are sharing a garden. I have to go to weed it, but even that's nice 'cause it gets me away and I can do the things that I want to do. I just love being outside. I love doing it.

The people who I met up north are very, very creative and they're spiritualists of some sort. They're all into some sort of therapy like that, and it's such a different way of life. It's very creative and it's something I never, ever felt like I wanted to be involved with but now I find it very, very interesting. So I've been sort of dabbling in this and learning to meditate and just doing things for myself. Really, I've got a long way to go. But I'm a very, very spiritualistic person anyway.

She never got much out of Alanon spiritually. There is a religious background there, but she draws a distinction between religion and spirituality.

I mean spiritualism is totally, totally different from any type of religion that you could have. And I feel very, very much in tune with my higher power and I'm really working on that and I think that's what it's going to take to make me the person that I need to be so that I don't keep falling into these stupid traps and coming up with the same type of men.

Abusive relationships, Beth figures, are easy to find. She doesn't think she could make it through another one, though. 'Two are my limit here,' she says. She has made a lot of acquaintances through groups of various kinds – co-dependent groups, AA, drug-related organizations – and she feels for those people and can understand where they are.

But I really don't want to spend the rest of my life making that distinction about whether we're going to be able to make it or not and having to go that whole route around where I still have to walk on eggs or whatever to make sure that someone else is getting what they need. I don't want to do that any more.

It was hard for her to do, but she has taken herself off the answering line for Alanon. There are other things she would like to be exploring now. She has recently been seeing a holistic healer and she is building a new sense of who she is. For example, she is reading books by Louise Hay, who writes about natural healing.

And [I'm] into the natural types of healing and the holistic healer I go to for holistic healing in Guelph [is] excellent at getting beyond the surface stuff that I know I'm working on. But when I go up there to her, if there's a problem somewhere and I say, 'Well I thought I dealt with that, I thought I was really working on it, I'm getting so much better,' she'll say, 'Yeah, well you have at this level, but, you know, it just hasn't gone beyond that. You're still surface.' I'm saying it but I'm not feeling it and getting it down into the conscious, the unconscious.

I do my meditation with a crystal. It's just such a comfortable place. I'm so surprised. To take all this stuff in your stride and just sort of float through there like I belong. It's just so new to me. It's like life is just beginning now. They say life begins at 40 – I'm a couple years over that. It's amazing after your kids have grown up and you've gone through those kinds of things, and you have a chance to get on your own and do some things for yourself and get back to it again, 'cause you lose that.

You lose parts of yourself because obviously your main focus isn't you. So it's kind of nice and I kind of like it the way it is now.

One of Beth's challenges in her recovery has been learning to say 'No.' She had to learn to stop trying to solve other people's problems or take on their responsibilities.

I've always done that. The first reaction whenever I go see somebody, whether it be a counsellor or whatever, is, 'Whew! You take on everybody right from the word go.' I mean if you have a problem, I don't just help you solve it, I get right in your body and take over!

I've spent my whole entire life worrying about someone else and what they do, [what] they are feeling, all those things. What I've learned is that you can't do for somebody else what you can't do for yourself; and although I was doing it and somebody benefited from it, it wasn't always for the right reasons, you know.

She has found that she often helped people in order to get out of doing something else, or out of habit, or to impress somebody. Now when she doesn't feel comfortable with doing something, she says 'No.' That way

*she won't be doing something while resenting all the time that she is
doing it.*

Was saying 'No' a hard thing to learn?

Terrible. It took me a long time, a lot of practice. I have
been practising 'No.' I mean I said the word 'No' I'd bet you
thousands of times just to prove I could say it, because it
was always a fact that, 'Just ask Beth. When she opens her
mouth, "Yes" comes out.' And it was so bad that it was a
joke. Everybody I work with, everybody that knows me
knows that, 'Just ask Beth, her mouth opens and "Yes" comes
out.'

*And it is getting easier as time goes by. Some of the concepts Beth learned
in Alanon she has made into tools to help her cope and recover.*

I'm really trying to live one day at a time. A lot of the things
I've learned in the Alanon programme, I've used. I go to
work every morning one day at a time. I really, I guess,
changed my life around. And I don't regret anything that's
ever happened in my life. It sounds crazy. I had to be there
to get here. And I think when you can live with that
concept, it doesn't matter. As long as I've done the best I
could do today. If somebody takes me out and runs me over
with a truck tomorrow and I haven't left any unfinished
business, you know, I've done what I can do to make my
point. I think what bothered me so much about Jayne and
putting things off like that is what would happen if I wasn't
here tomorrow.

Alanon I think was the first bright light at the time
when I really needed it. And even though I don't agree with
everything, it's like any other programme, you take what
you want and put the rest back. But the concepts that it
taught me to begin with taught me, number one, about my
kids and Brittany especially. You know, to 'let go and let
God', 'live and let live', like all those neat little [Alcoholic
Anonymous] slogans they have when you're going through
life and you're living it one hour at a time or one minute
at a time, when life is just that bad. And it has been.

*She has learned to use everything she can to get through the day. All
those little slogans, prayers and reminders.*

Sometimes I said them hundreds of times in a day just to get through a day. You know, so you could crawl into bed at night and hopefully shut your mind off, which very seldom ever happened but it was a day over with. And I think a lot of the concepts in that programme were just excellent.

Beth has changed. She sees herself as very different to how she was at the time of the disclosures.

Oh, it's just so different. I can't believe even just, like I say, when I went into counselling two years ago, I [wasn't] even a portion of the person I am now. It's amazing when you stop to think, you know? At that point I was so [overwhelmed by] all the problems that were around me and I was so tensed up and stressed all the time. I was laughing and doing the things that I've always done, it's just there was no feeling behind it. I didn't have any feeling for me.

She didn't like herself then, wasn't comfortable with herself, didn't want to be the person she was and didn't like her attitude even about her own children. Now she finds her world open and anything is possible. The standards she lives by are her own and she can change if she wants to.
She has taken up canoeing and swimming. She has been experiencing nature and farm life and is exploring her spirituality. During the previous interview Beth had given indications that she had seen the possibility of a new world opening up for her. Now, a year later, she has actually made some of that happen.

And it's just great and I love it. And I'm sure that there's a lot more in store for me. I don't know, I guess I just have a real feeling about myself, a lot more confidence in myself and there isn't anything that I can't master if I want to do it. And I don't think I've ever had that confidence before. Even these last couple of years, although I was barrelling ahead and doing what I had to do, it wasn't necessarily what I wanted to do. It was those things that you sort of make an outline for yourself and [that] you have to accomplish because they are the things that have to be done in order to get through this. But now since I'm over that hump and I'm basically through that, now it's what I want to do. And I can do anything. There are a lot of things that I can't do and I wouldn't feel comfortable doing, but for the most part things that are within reason for me, I can do.

Was there a specific turning point for her?

I don't know, there was never a real line. Like I said, Jayne was the last one. And I had put her off. There was a time when I reached one plateau, where I had done most of the things that I had to do. And this was the last one, talking to Conrad again, going to his counsellor, making sure Jayne was told. Those are the last ones and I think that I had reached a point before that and I was almost comfortable there.

But there was that nagging feeling that you are not finished yet and you're going to have to do it. And I really procrastinated as long as it was possible for me to do it. So now I think, today, mailing the letter was very difficult for me, because once I'd mailed it, it was done. You can't take back what's in the mail.

4 Fay

Stories normally have a beginning, middle and end. Fay's story, however, communicates a feeling of being continuously in the middle. I spent a great deal of time inside of Fay's story growing more confused and distraught at the unsolvable nature of her dilemma.

Fay is a woman in her late 30s. She has two daughters: Alicia, 17 years old at the time of our first meeting, and Marcia, 14. When we first met, Fay was living with her eldest daughter after a recent separation from her common-law husband, Rick. She had separated from Marcia's and Alicia's natural father more than five years earlier. The children then lived with their father and stepmother for four years. Marcia was placed in foster care for six months after that and then both daughters moved in with Fay.

Six weeks after moving in Marcia disclosed that almost a year earlier Rick had touched her breast. The police and Family and Children's Services became involved and Rick was charged with sexual interference and sentenced to 18 months' probation. At the time of the interview about six months remained of his sentence.

The continuing high stress from the events surrounding the disclosure caused Fay to quit her job and she has been unemployed now for the last nine months. She takes medication to alleviate her depression.

Stress was also one reason Fay had left the children with their father for four years. She didn't feel she could look after them and give them what they needed because of her high level of stress. But she didn't like her choice.

> I felt guilty for the four years the girls were with their Dad. I'd see them when I could and everything, but I wanted them to be with me. Only, I knew I couldn't take care of them. And when I sent them [to be] with their father I knew that. Well, I guess we were going for counselling then too with my daughter, Marcia; we had her in counselling when she was very young. And I just knew that I couldn't let the kids make a choice between their father and I. The same

as where I am [choosing between my husband and daughter], and I really didn't want to make that choice either. It was better for me to make it than to have them in the middle to choose between us. So I just couldn't let them. I couldn't burden them with that: that's a big choice. You can't make a kid choose. They were nine and twelve, I think. And they loved both of us no matter what, so I thought, 'I'll make the decision,' even though it was tough.

She had more tough choices to make after the disclosure: who was to stay and who was to go?

It was a rotten time. Very confusing, a lot of turmoil. A lot of unanswered questions, I guess. I still wonder. It's too bad you have to take sides, you have to choose. I don't know, it puts you in an awkward position. Oh yeah. Your head's just spinning all the time. It gets like that sometimes now, but not quite as bad, not quite as often.

Fay was left with no way out. She had to choose between two undesirable options – to lose either her daughter or her husband. Unable to choose, Fay vacillated between the two.

First I took my daughter's side, then I took my common-law's side, then I took my daughter's side. I am really confused. I don't know what to believe. It was sexual interference, not sexual assault; it was touching of the breast for a few seconds. Now my daughter says that he touched her and he's saying that she took his hand and put it on her, and knowing the kind of daughter I have, I really don't know what to believe.

She felt she had cause to doubt her daughter's side of the story.

It's just so hard to know who to believe. But my ex-husband, everybody, they all said, well he said that she [Marcia] tried to split them up: he and his new wife. There were just so many things against my daughter that it was so hard to take her side.

Fay loved both her common-law husband and her daughter, but they couldn't be in the house together.

In fact, when Marcia would come home in the middle of the night and Rick was here, I would lock her in her bedroom. Actually one night I locked her room from the outside with a hook and eye and I locked my room where Rick was and I slept on the couch with my eyes open. I felt like a warden. In fact I was up at 6 o'clock in the morning, so I only got a couple of hours, I don't even think I went to sleep. Marcia came in about 4 and I know I was up doing laundry at 6, but I don't think I slept. It bothered me. I thought, 'I don't know who or what happened, I'll lock them both in. If one has to get out to go to the bathroom they'll have to knock on the door and I'll let them out. And I'll be the guard.' Oh, I felt terrible.

Children's Aid made her choose between the two and, reluctantly, she did.

Well, there was so much confusion. I found out the 19th, a Thursday, and by the Monday I had made up my mind that Marcia was leaving and I've just been tossing everything back and forth and going crazy. I don't know, your head gets – I don't think you know which way you're coming or going. You don't know what to do. A lot of confusion. You don't know what you're doing, really. As far as I'm concerned, you shouldn't have to make decisions. You shouldn't be put on that spot.

The decisions Fay made weigh heavily on her and she remains uncertain of whether she did the right thing. She has done a good deal of reading on the subject, but is unimpressed.

They think they know. And quite often the mother is to blame. And it's the mother that's in the middle and, I don't know, I feel that Rick's dealing with what's happened. Fine. That's OK for him. Marcia, she ran away. Some day I hope she'll deal with it though. Myself, I'm dealing with what's happened between them, I'm dealing with each individually, worrying … I just feel like everything's put on me and that I'm carrying a load of bricks around. Because I'm so confused about a lot of things right now, I don't know who I am. I don't know if I want Rick any more … There's so much going on and the Mom always has to make all the choices.

Her self-esteem plummeted and a few months after the disclosure, overburdened by stress, Fay quit her job.

Just everything. The courts, not having anything settled. I don't know. Just so much. I ended up very depressed. Well, I still am but I'm on medication and going to lots of counselling. That [the disclosure] was October and I quit about three months later. I just couldn't handle it any more. I had too many calls to make and Children's Aid [was involved]. I was keeping in close contact with them. Police. Well, my daughter was on the streets then too.

At the same time, Fay was unsure of whether Rick may, in fact, have sexually abused her daughter.

I'm scared. I'm wondering if I've made a bad choice here and yet I guess if Rick and I love each other enough, it'll happen. We'll get back together. I might have pushed him away. I was pushing him away when he was living here. I wasn't being that nice to him. I wasn't paying attention to him. I didn't want him sitting by me, I was verbally nasty. I wasn't very nice to him ... I think everything got put together. I didn't know where anything was coming from or going. I was too confused about stuff.

Fay herself had been sexually abused as a child and she wondered how that might have affected her relationships. Was she treating Rick fairly?

I'm wondering if I'm punishing him for that. Some day I'm hoping, through all my counselling, that I will find that out, because I trusted him. If he's done this, he's lost my trust and I just don't know how I feel any more. I don't know if I love him any more, I don't know if that trust is there. Sometimes I feel it is, other times it isn't ... But it really makes it hard on me and he only got 18 months' probation – I felt it was fair at the time but now I think he should've gone to jail. I think he didn't learn anything, but ... I can't believe that a judge that doesn't even know the person, how he could make his decision, because I'm not even sure about my decision really. Well, I gave him a lot of evidence against my daughter, which didn't help. At that time I was on that side and now I'm confused, I'm not sure what I want, where I side, and I've felt bad ever since then. I've thought, 'What if Marcia was telling the truth?' I don't know, I'm not sure if I need to know but I feel I need to know, I really do. It's tearing me apart.

Fay decided to separate from Rick to give her a chance to sort out her life. Ironically, unable to choose either Rick's or Marcia's side, she ends up with neither.

> Right now I think I need to know me, to find myself because I don't even know who I am. I was sexually abused as a child and I've never dealt with that, so I'm joining a survivors' group. I just need to know myself right now. Rick and I have separated so I can have the time to do that. That was my decision. I just felt that I wasn't getting anywhere as far as finding myself because he has an influence on [me] of course and I thought, 'I need him as far away as possible so that I can do that,' and he was willing to give me that space. I don't know for how long, though.

At least this way Fay doesn't have to take care of anybody. For a change she can look after herself first. Like many women, she has difficulty putting herself first. She sees this as due to something in her upbringing, a certain kind of conditioning by her mother and stepfathers. They were always putting her down, she related; she was never good enough for anything. When she did get sexual attention from her stepfathers, this seemed positive in comparison.

> At least I thought I was getting more positive attention from the stepfathers, only it was sexual abuse. It's pretty confusing but it seemed to be a more positive attention. Plus I had clothes bought for me. I had spending money. They didn't call me a little bitch or say I was a rotten kid or I was stupid or all those things. So it felt like it was positive attention, at least I think [so]. It's pretty confusing actually. But someday I'll work this all out. And I actually think that when I start working on myself and my abuse that maybe that will help with Marcia's a little better.

Fay's experience of having a daughter who has been sexually abused has changed her views about her own mother. She wonders if it will help to talk to her mother about her abuse back in 1967. Her mother suspected something was going on and Fay's stepfather was charged with abusing Fay at one point. Fay was so afraid to testify against him that she lied in court and denied anything ever happened. The case was dismissed, Fay's stepfather was freed and Fay was sent to a training school for troublesome girls.

Worst thing I could have done in my life because I moved
to training school in T. Training school for eleven months
for not admitting because I felt that it was my fault, that I
was the reason that the abuse happened, that I asked for
it. Anyway, [there was] just a lot of guilt and I blamed myself
all my life. It's interfered with my life as far as my marriage,
my common-law relationship, just my whole life period [are
concerned]. It's interfered here and there but I'm glad it's
well known now. I've told my children, 'Don't ever be
afraid to tell me,' and they know it's happened to me.
Well, I've always told them not to be afraid. I've warned
them against aunts, uncles, grandparents, anybody, because
I know, and I guess probably from reading a lot too, I know
it's always been someone close to me, that I've trusted
[who's been the abuser].

*Considering the disruptive effect the disclosure by her daughter had on
her family and on her, Fay can understand why a child might not want
to disclose she was being sexually abused.*

I think the reason why I didn't want to tell, [and what] makes
it very hard for a child now, is the breakup in the family.
That proved it when my daughter made the disclosure:
everybody had to make choices, especially myself. I don't
know what it would have done to my Mom and that's
probably why I didn't tell her. And seeing what it did to
me when Marcia told me, I'm glad I didn't tell my Mom
and I don't know if I will. It's something I'll have to work
out. In a way I want to talk to my Mom about it, let her
know that I know that it's not her fault. She may have
suspected, but it was up to me to tell. Kids just didn't tell.
It wasn't even talked about back then. It was pretty hush-
hush. That's why I'm glad it's out today, that kids can feel
free to tell. But the way they go about the disclosure, there's
got to be something they can do different.

*One thing she would like to find out from her mother is whether she
had been abused in her time. Her mother was not a happy person and
had a hard life. Perhaps she, too, carried a similar burden. How many
more generations of abuse might there have been?*

By the sounds of things, child abuse has been around for
years and I think that my Mom was probably abused and
is going through the same thing that I went through, only

she is in her 50s now, you know, almost 60. Never had the support and the help she should've needed or that she did need. I'm glad that there's more available today, and there's still not enough. I think if my Mom had've had the counselling and everything I did, she would've looked at life a little different.

Fay doesn't blame her mother for anything that has happened in her life. She feels that her mother looked after her as best she was able, just as Fay cared for her children. And she would like to assure her Mom that she was not a 'bad' Mom. Fay feels she has an advantage because she knows sexual abuse is wrong. If her mother knew what she knew now, things would have been different.

But I just cannot believe that there is so much abuse out there and I thought that I was the only one, of course. When I was growing up I thought that I was the only one. Mind you, I said I'd never let it happen to my kids. I always said that.

Fay's relationship with Marcia is a difficult one.

She doesn't talk to me any more. She's very angry with me and I don't know why. Because I'm the one so far that has helped her. Anytime she's needed help, I've helped her. This happened, well, a year ago, pretty close to a year. At least eleven months. And she's been through a lot. She's on the streets.

I was there for her all the time and I'm still there. She can call me or come in at 4 o'clock in the morning, it doesn't matter. Sometimes, most of the time, she treats me like dirt, but I understand that she has a lot of anger and I would like her to be able to talk to me or be angry with me, whatever it takes. I'm going through a lot of counselling to help me with that. To be able to cope with that.

On the one hand, Fay tries to support her daughter and to get the system to work to protect her and work for her. On the other hand, it was her decision that Marcia leave home. The contradiction in her behaviour is an indication that Fay could see no way to keep the family intact and maintain good relations with both her daughter and her common-law husband.

The system wasn't working for Marcia. After the disclosure she kept running away, living on the streets. A judge, who was frustrated with

Marcia's behaviour, gave responsibility for Marcia to her boyfriend, Todd, although Fay retained legal guardianship. Because Todd had previously abused Marcia, Fay then went for help to local MPs and other politicians. Her complaint was brought up in the House of Commons at one point, but nothing came of it. None of Fay's efforts resulted in increased safety for Marcia. Within weeks of the judge's decision, Todd began beating Marcia again. On previous occasions the police had not pressed charges against Todd because of the likelihood that Marcia would deny that he had beaten her. But now Marcia did charge him, and then called her mother.

> Anytime she calls I'm there. So I went there. That was to the [street kids'] programme, and when I got there, I talked to the girl in charge and then Marcia came in shortly after and she says, 'I'm dropping the charges. Todd threatened to kill me if I don't drop the charges.' So I thought, 'Great.' Anyway, I stayed with her for a while and went over to the police station and I talked to the officer that took the call.

Fay told him there had been previous beatings, severe enough to take Marcia to hospital. She thought that this time things were going to change because Marcia had got up the courage to press charges. But Marcia was afraid and the police let her drop the charges. Fay was hopeful that at least the police had on record that there had been a call. If there was another one they would be able to take it more seriously.

A local organization for street kids has been Marcia's only continuous point of contact since the disclosure. Fay has watched her daughter's health decline. She estimates that Marcia has lost 40–50 pounds since she began living on the streets and lives with the fear that her daughter might die on the streets.

> Marcia had been beat up by Todd one night and I phoned the police at 5 o'clock in the morning because I was trying to find her. She had been over at Alicia's boyfriend's parents' that night, or was going to come over and didn't, but Alicia and her boyfriend had seen them and she had a black eye for sure. All I knew is that she was hurt and nobody knew where she was. So 5 o'clock in the morning I was still up and I thought, 'I am going to phone the police and have them go get her.'

Fay met with the school board to try and keep Marcia in some kind of school programme.

We made all the arrangements, she started school. Todd beat her up that night. She went to school the next day with a black eye. They asked her how it happened, I think. Maybe they didn't have to ask and she just told them. As far as I know she just told them that Todd had done it and then I thought, 'Why was this not reported?' And I took her to the hospital and she reported that her boyfriend beat her up, but it was not reported and I thought that the hospital, teachers, anybody that knew of anything about abuse was supposed to report it. She was in school [a total of] two days.

She told them the boyfriend did it, so when I went to the police station and told them, they said that she has to lay the charge and I said, 'I don't think so.' And that's when they gave me the story that, yeah, she could go to court and say he didn't do it. She told the school and she told the hospital [about the beating]. I don't know, I just think that they're pawning everything off on everybody else. I'm the one doing all the running around, all the calling. On the night that I did take them, the police, to look for Marcia at 5 in the morning we found out she wasn't there. There was Todd, this other boy and two girls and the police removed the two girls and told me that my daughter wasn't there. [The police officer] also told me that I should go and take a course in tough love.

What did she think about that advice?

I wasn't too thrilled. I thought, 'I love my kid. I'm not going to just have her out on the streets.' This was winter time. She had nowhere to live, they were living in caves and everything. She'd come home black, so filthy, smelling, I'd let her in, I didn't care what time of night it was. Let her in, give her a shower, something to eat, put her in bed.

On those occasions when Marcia phoned or came home, Fay would phone Family and Children's Services or the police and have them pick her up and take her to a safe place. She wasn't safe at her boyfriend's. At one point there was a hearing regarding assault charges against Todd, but Marcia didn't show. The judge issued a court order directing all involved, including the police, to find her and get her into court.

I found Marcia. And I feel like a real meany. Like, here I am turning in my child because I couldn't get her off the streets. I needed help to do that. Anyway, I told the police that Marcia would phone me in trust and I would have to phone the police and say where she was. Go and get her. Everything was put back on me. [Family and Children's Services], police, everybody. I was always in the middle, in the middle of everything. I don't even know if it was in the middle, I just felt that everything was put on me and that I didn't have any support. I just didn't like to have to turn in my own child.

There was another thing that, when the disclosure came about, I had gone over to Children and Family Services and the detective that was there asked me to go home and confront Rick – ME, as if I was the police or the lawyer, whoever. I was the one that had to come home and ask Rick and then take Rick up to the police station and that's exactly what I did. I felt like I was being the lawyer or the police. That I was doing their job. That's not my job. I just really didn't have the support I needed. I don't know. Maybe they didn't believe Marcia. I didn't like that at all and I'm glad that Rick was OK with it. Because he could have been very angry with me. Who knows?

Taking into consideration Fay's description of Marcia's childhood, especially her early sexualized behaviour towards men, there is a definite possibility that Marcia, like her mother, was sexually abused in the past. Marcia's childhood is over and Fay can feel her loss.

You'd think she's probably 30, 35 for all she's been through in the last year. Oh it's terrible [to watch]. All I want is for her to come home and I know, I know she can't even be a kid, and that's all I've ever wanted, for her to have a regular child life because I didn't have one and that's all I wanted for my kids, to be kids. To have fun. I don't know, I just don't understand the system.

What could have been done that would have been helpful to her?

I'm not sure. I wish that I wasn't put on the spot and had to make the choices that I did. That was a lot of pressure. It's still a lot of pressure, so it's not over yet. I don't know if it will ever end, actually. It's a crisis time. For some reason it doesn't seem like the family should be separated. Common-law or otherwise. It just seems like it's such a bad time that that's when the family needs each other. Why

make them make choices? I know, I guess, it's for both the
offender and the victims, and yet things would have turned
out a lot different if I didn't have to choose.

*Fay is a survivor of sexual abuse, as is her daughter and, quite possibly,
her own mother. She is caught in a history of abuse and in a situation
which has no clear solution, no right response. She has spent a year
trying to reconcile conflicting thoughts and actions and to clear her mind
of a lot of confusion – without much success. She still feels caught in
the middle.*

The second meeting

*By the second interview Fay's confusion and depression had improved
and several positive changes had taken place in her life. Marcia was
now living at home for the second time and Fay felt strong enough to
handle it (a previous attempt had failed). Fay clearly felt more in
charge of her life. How did she come to feel this way?*

Learning that I didn't have to be a victim any more. I
think that's really what it comes down to, because I always
let everybody else tell me what to do.

*When Marcia came home the first time, Fay discovered that both she
and Marcia had changed. She had come to see herself as having been
victimized by her daughter's behaviour as well as by that of others. She
would not put up with manipulation from anybody – she asked Marcia
to leave.*

Only now I know that I can have control of my own life.
And, I don't know, I kicked – I shouldn't say kicked – her
out. I found that she had changed so much. I guess that's
what it was. And that I really couldn't live with her.
 Her telling me what to do. I thought, 'No way.' So
anyway, I was glad to see her go the second time. But the
first time it was something I couldn't control. I guess
control is the right word. Like my hands were tied and I
had no choice in what happened. Then Alicia said to me
when Marcia left the second time, 'Why did you let her come
home in the first place?' And I said I needed to do that for
me because of the way I was feeling months ago.

Fay feels that living on the street has made Marcia more manipulative than before and that she has become less inclined to put up with it.

Both Fay's daughters have boyfriends and she worries about their relationships, both of which are controlled by their boyfriends. It is painful to watch. She has been a good teacher.

> And actually I just want to see [Alicia] out of her relationship, because her boyfriend is very controlling, too controlling. He's a year younger! I can't believe the control he has, and Marcia's boyfriend also. But they've always seen me in that type of relationship, so I think they think that's normal. I'm trying to tell them now that it's not: this is the way it's supposed to be. I can just see the both of them getting married and being where I was. Their self-esteem is very low. I can't stand [to watch] it and I can't tell them. I guess they have to learn the same as I did. Really.

The confusion that Fay once felt and the anger towards the judge who 'gave' Marcia to her abusive boyfriend has shifted and has given way to understanding.

> Things are a lot clearer now. I don't know, I guess there was just so much happening and a lot of things I didn't understand. People's decisions that were being made. Like the judge giving Marcia's boyfriend permission to be responsible for her and stuff like that. I think that the judge just couldn't see. I think he felt he didn't really have a lot of choices, because Marcia was going to do anything she wanted to do anyway. But now that she's back, things will hopefully get changed, she'll get her life straightened out.

Marcia no longer sees her old boyfriend. That relationship lasted for about a year, during which there were regular beatings and there were drugs and alcohol. But Marcia realized the situation she was in and got out. Fay considers this a positive step.

> I guess she was away from him for about a month and then came home. But she said to me when she left, after she had been home for six months, she didn't want to be here. She was here because everybody said she should be here. And this time she says she wants to be here. And she's going to counselling. So, that's a good sign on her part. Because she's been saying, 'No, I don't want counselling.'

Marcia now has another boyfriend.

That's been for the last six months. He's controlling and stuff, but it's a little more positive, I guess. He doesn't believe in hitting her and stuff like that.

Fay now feels it is an individual's decision to remain a victim or to step out of that position. When Fay considers her own personal changes and increased ability to make decisions, she looks at her daughters and sees their victim role as a choice.

I can see them being victims for as long as they allow theirselves to be victims. I think that's really what it comes down to. 'Cause you do have choices. You don't always know that, though. I guess things have to get to rock bottom. You say, 'I just can't take this any more,' or 'I can't handle this. This isn't the way I want my life to be.' And then you start looking for ways to go.

Can a victim 'choose' to be a victim when she is unaware there are other options, I wonder?

Fay has frequently mentioned the word 'control' and she has developed her own beliefs about control and how patterns of control develop in relationships. She has come to the conclusion that either you want to be controlled or you want to control someone else. This is a point of view she never held before and one she acquired through counselling and listening to other people.

And I can see all those things now, you know, in other people. Where before I thought I was the only one.

I'm just hoping that I can – I don't know what the right word is – that I will know if there's an abuser. I don't want my kids to ever be in that position again. Mind you, I think they know that they have control over that. And if it happens, I think they'd come to me. And yet that really is tough to say. Because if I was in a relationship that I wanted to work, and they liked that person [even if he was abusing them], I don't know if they would [tell me]. They've seen me so unhappy, right? I'm not so sure. I hope so. I guess I really need to get that point across. I'm not sure that this is a good sign, but at times I look at any man as a potential abuser. I don't know if I got those words right. You know, like I just don't trust anyone any more?

Fay looks at a number of things differently.

I actually think I know, or am gradually beginning to know, what I want and what I want to do with my life. What direction I want it to go. So, I'm dating.

Well, I guess being sexually abused, being physically and mentally abused at home as a child, I think I grew up too fast. And ... got married at 18, started my family at 20. I just never got to do the things I should have done and this is what I'm trying to tell my kids. You know: date, don't go steady. Well, they're both going steady. I just think they're too young to do that. And I did say to Marcia yesterday, because we talk about me dating, 'When you're my age, you might be going through the same thing as far as this dating stuff [is concerned], if you don't do it now.' I'm roller-skating, doing lots of things I should have done when I was a kid. So it's kinda neat actually. I love it.

In a way Fay feels like an adolescent again, and she talks about dating in that way.

I want someone that cares about me. I guess it's more like wanting to go steady, and yet I don't want to go steady. But I want all the benefits of going steady, I guess.

I don't want someone that's going to be telling me what to do. So I want to take my time. Not rush into anything. I don't want to put myself in any position that I could be the victim again.

Fay is well aware how easy it would be to fall back into another controlling relationship.

It is easy. You want someone to take care of you. You want the love and everything. I know a big thing is you have to love yourself first. And I never knew what that meant.

What does she think this means now?

Well, it's self-esteem. I've learned to like myself and that I'm worth a lot more than I ever thought. I don't know. I just had a low opinion of myself. I was always told as a child that I was more or less worth nothing, that I was stupid, no good.

Yeah. I'm really experimenting. I guess before, I never had the choices. You know, I usually had to do as I was told. But now I say, 'If I want to do it I'm going to do it.' And I won't let anyone tell me I can't do it.

The changes in Fay are noticeable to other people, including her family, friends and members of the women's group she attends.

We got together last night, the Mothers' Group. We had a potluck dinner and I hadn't seen Laura maybe since Christmas or something. And she says, 'Boy you look good, you sound good, there's a big difference in you.' And I like it. People have noticed, yeah. And myself too. In fact I've had people say to me at roller-skating – and I see them two or three times a week – 'You're always happy.' And I [say], 'Yeah.' Yeah. I don't think I was ever so happy in all my life.

Well, I've probably changed. I've learned that life is what you make it and that other people don't have the right to [control it]. My moods always depended on the people that I was with. So if I was around negative people, that wasn't good. So now I pick and choose the people I'm with and I'm usually around pretty positive people. It really depends a lot on yourself. If you're down I think you attract that kind of people.

Fay's sense of herself is very different from what it was and she has adopted a certain philosophy of life which has made the experience of the last few years more understandable.

I just feel that everything in my life has happened for a reason and when it's happened it's been the time for it. So I just take one day at a time and whatever happens, happens.

I know I hate seeing abuse of any kind. Why, I don't know. I think what it comes down to is we're learning from this. And it's happening for a reason. It's probably the same thing as anything else. Why does anything in life happen? Am I turning religious? I don't know.

If I had my way there would never be any abuse in this world, but I know there's got to be a reason it's happening. And I don't think there would be a solution, that it would just stop. But I think from what I've understood now, it's been around for centuries. It's sure a lot of other people would like to do something about it, but I think it's always going to be there. All we can do is be there to help people get through it. I always thought there was going to be a cure, but I don't think there is.

But now I think it's a miracle. I'm thinking more. I think it's something that we have to learn to cope with, help people get through. I think it's always going to be there.

And probably society has a lot to do with this, but unless everybody goes for counselling and it works, people's way of thinking isn't going to change. My way of thinking has really changed. That's scary but it's good. I wish everybody could go [through] what I've gone through. The outcome is fantastic. I would've never thought that this could ever happen. And yet I know, like with Marcia and Alicia, I'd like them both to go for counselling. It's a decision they have to make and want to go or it won't work. For example, perpetrators – we can make them go to counselling but if they don't want to go, I don't think it's going to change them at all. They're still going to be that person, that potential abuser. Yeah, it really has a lot to do with their outlook on life and how they feel about themselves.

And that's the same as us being victims. If we stay in that situation and we don't do anything about it, then it's going to be the same.

Fay is seeing men again and she is applying her new understanding of the world to her relationships with men.

What I have found, and I think it's right, for one thing you really have to get to know a person and I guess this is where it comes. Knowing yourself and loving yourself, all those things, all that comes into play because when you have all that, at least what I've learned and I've found out, is that you can see those qualities in other people. Because men I've gone out with that have those qualities do not try to control me. Well, their self-esteem is good. And I think, at least I hope I'm right, people with those qualities think enough of themselves that they don't need to abuse. So I think that they're the right kind of person I need to find. And I think an abuser is someone that doesn't have the self-esteem, is controlling, is abusive in other ways.

Fay has never really dated, it's all pretty new to her and she likes it. It feels good. It's something she needs to do for herself and she is beginning to know her needs and how to fulfil them.

When I need a hug, I just ask for it. Before, I didn't even know I needed a hug. You know, just little things that I think should be natural. And what I've needed, I've wanted to tell people what I need. Before, I wouldn't have said anything. In fact, I would've put up with it: abuse, verbal abuse, controlling, this type of thing. Where now I say, 'Hey, wait a minute. I have a say in this and this is what I want and this is what I need.' And if they don't like it then that's their problem. But before, there [would have been] no way. I always went with the flow ... Actually this is good. I have to do this every once in a while. Talk to a counsellor or someone and go over what's happened.

At our first interview she was taking anti-depressants. Is she still taking them?

I went off them around Christmas [eight months earlier]. Took myself off them. I guess my body just figured that I didn't need them any more. It was just so natural. I guess with all my counselling, all that support I had. I didn't think about it or anything. I guess my body just said, 'You don't need them any more,' and I just kinda stopped taking them. I thought that was kinda weird. I thought, 'How come I'm forgetting to take my pills?' And then I wouldn't go to the doctor to get more.

Before, Fay always felt somebody needed to make decisions for her. She was often under someone's control, being told she was stupid and, by implication, incapable of making choices. She knows now she can make decisions on her own and feel good about them. She has ideas on how decisions ought to be made.

It takes time. There are some things, like an everyday thing maybe, like whether you're going to go to the park or whether you're going to go to the beach or whatever. Going away for the weekend, those types of things, you can make a decision [on] right away. Something that's life-threatening or whatever, well those kind of things take time. You can't make a snap decision. And when they involve other people – I don't know.

The thing is too, admitting things to yourself. Or confirming things. I don't know what it is but eventually it does come to a decision and you know exactly what it is you want at that time. But until then you're just mulling it around.

What I've experienced, I think that's what life is. It's something that you have to go through to know. It's knowledge. I'm sure that I went through this for many reasons. I've learned a lot from it and a lot of different things. Months ago, there's no way I could've said this, and I didn't want to go through it but I had to. It's not something I would want anyone to go through, but I think that we've gone through these things to learn from it. Because in fact while I was going through my counselling, and I'm not so sure now because I've kind of put it on the back burner, I thought of being a counsellor or at least volunteering. I've gone through this for a reason and I'm sure it's to help other people. While you're going through it, though, it's hell. And you have to go through it. Same as trying to tell my kids, don't do this or don't do that because this will happen. They still have to go through it to learn, no matter how much I don't want them to. Like their boyfriends controlling them and stuff like this. It's just a learning process, I guess.

Were things as clear as that at the time?

No way! And you don't want to be there. But I've just found, and especially with me learning a whole lot of things and a new way of life, I could have never experienced it if I hadn't gone through it. I would've never known. I could never have gone from the bad to the good. I guess the only thing I could say is things do get better and it will be worth it in the end, but it is rough.

5 June

June was 32 years old at the time of our first interview. She had divorced her husband, Jim, and was living in a townhouse complex with her daughter, Pam, who had just turned five. June's mother had lost her job some months ago and was now also living with them.

June grew up in a family with seven kids, at least several of whom were sexually and physically abused. The message she grew up with, and one that still surrounds her, is that sexual abuse is normal – just part of growing up. Only three of June's sisters have much to do with her. Alice is June's elder sister and the one to whom Pam eventually disclosed being sexually abused. Maggie, her youngest sister, also has a daughter, Karen, a couple of years older than Pam. At the time of disclosure, Maggie was living with her common-law husband, Garth, whom she eventually married. Suzanne is the second youngest sister and although she was not involved with Pam's disclosure, she figures in the various conflicts that arose after it.

June started to suspect sexual abuse shortly after her daughter turned three. She had been taking Pam to see a doctor about once every two weeks for lower abdominal pains and yeast infections, but no one made anything of it. Perhaps Pam had a narrow urethra. Some tests were done. Pam had some allergies, perhaps they were the cause of the yeast infections. Then, on different occasions, Pam and her then five-and-a-half-year-old cousin were found undressed and touching each other's genitalia. There was something about the play between Pam and Karen that disturbed June.

> I started noticing the fear between Pam and Karen and the play. Karen's words; they weren't normal for a normal child. My sister kept saying: 'It's just child's play,' and I says: 'Look! Karen's being molested and she's molesting Pam. Find out where it's coming from.'

Pam was wetting her bed and just frantic with fear of Karen sometimes, crying that she didn't want to go see her. June just thought she was in a bad mood or, as she puts it, being a brat. In retrospect, she feels that her frequent visits to the doctor and the type of complaint involved should have alerted a professional to the possibility of sexual abuse: 'They were trying to find the obvious, something obvious rather than looking behind closed doors.'

The sisters started to look for a perpetrator. One weekend they met at Alice's place in London, Ontario. Maggie announced that Pam had disclosed to Alice that Saturday morning, while they were shopping, that her Dad had been touching her. Alice called the police, who prepared to lay charges of child sexual abuse against Jim. Pam was almost four years old at the time of this disclosure.

June had to press for action when it appeared that there would be delays because the person who would be in charge of the case was on holiday. Also there were potential delays because some paperwork needed to be transferred from one police station to another. Almost three days later it was arranged that after Jim got home from work at 6 pm on Monday, he would be arrested. On the advice of the police, June and Pam went out for supper so that the arrest could be made in their absence. It was all supposed to be over by 7 pm.

> Well, we got home at 7:30. Who comes out to help unload the car? So he could sense something and they came about 15 minutes, half an hour later.

June feels that without her pushing the issue, the police 'would've sat on it'. While Jim was down at the police station she was told of homes and shelters for women in her situation.

> Why me? Pam's got allergies, she's got insecurities, I got to make sure I take the right toys, all her allergy foods. It's just, 'Why me?' And so, between phoning [local shelters] and the cop shop and – I don't know, I don't remember – he came home and packed his stuff. I [was] determined: 'I [won't] do anything, I'm not leaving.' I can be quite stubborn.

June found it difficult to cope with the ordeal that followed. She was responsible for getting herself and Pam to numerous appointments with doctors, psychiatrists, court, and Family and Children's Services.

> Well, I went on four months' leave of absence. I just couldn't concentrate. My mind was just all over. I'd be going

to an appointment and I'd find myself going to a different place because I had so many appointments and I just couldn't keep my head straight from the appointment book. And then the frustration. Nobody would take Pam.

Who in particular did she mean when she said 'nobody'?

Friends, family. I was over-reacting. 'She's going to point her finger at me, for wiping her,' or something. She was the plague. I was the plague.

The family and friends reacted to the disclosure by ostracizing June and her daughter and withdrawing their support. This was one of the more glaring examples of lack of support. Although she was not working at this point and was receiving welfare, June continued to take Pam to daycare.

I'm not supposed to take her [and] just in case, I had the doctor write me up a note to verify that I had to. But the day was spent running, trying to get things in order and even when I went back to work, I was off for an extra two weeks because I came down with pneumonia. I ended up in the hospital with a fever of 105 and nobody would drive me to the hospital. Some friends said, 'That's your problem. I can't, what will people think, me driving you to the hospital at 3 o'clock in the morning?' This was a male – [concerned about] what they would think.

Family and Children's Services told her she couldn't leave Pam with Jim's family, because they might leave her with Jim. She couldn't leave Pam with her family because of their history of abuse. They suggested instead a local agency providing relief childcare services for families in crisis. June was afraid to use their services in case there were children there with more problems than her child. She couldn't afford to pay a babysitter.

At the time of the disclosure June was already seeing a counsellor. She had been having frightening visions prior to the disclosure, and her counsellor afterwards suggested that perhaps she had been abused as a child and that witnessing the sexual acting out by the girls may have triggered memories from her past and actually helped her realize that the children's play was not normal play.

I would see myself stabbing Jim when we were making love or I would go in the drawer for a spoon and I would see the scissors, and my hand didn't move, but I saw my hand in my mind move and Pam's laying there with the scissors in her chest.

I never had a shower, it did not relax me. I had a bath, washed my hair lying down in the bathtub and then one night my hands were pushing my head under the water.

And I'd never go in to check Pam during the night when I got up to go to the washroom, and yet I'd always light a cigarette, go to the washroom and back to bed. One night, and this is all in the one week, I went to the washroom and I went a couple steps to Pam's bedroom door and I leaned against the doorjamb and started walking away and I glanced back and the bed's on fire. And yet the cigarette was in my hand, her bed wasn't on fire.

When she told Pam's counsellor of her visions, he reacted differently.

Dr L says I'm bullshitting: 'Why don't you admit it? You were trying suicide but you're too afraid to admit it. Your mind cannot do those things.' I found that oncoming car headlights hypnotized me and I'd just kind of be staring at them as they were coming towards me as I was driving, and I'd come to. But, I mean, he more or less told me that I was unconsciously trying to commit suicide but will not admit it. Oh he's an idiot, Dr L is, but [other professionals] could understand my mental unbalance. I just had no space, I couldn't breathe. Jim and Pam were just getting more and more demanding of me.

Dr L advised Family and Children's Services they should remove Pam from June's care because she was too unbalanced to be looking after a four-and-a-half-year-old. June had already met with Children's Aid on a number of occasions and they knew her. They made up their own minds and didn't take Dr L's advice.

But service providers such as Family and Children's Services are apprehensive about women like June. As she and her sisters were sexually abused as children, they may see her as indirectly responsible for the sexual abuse of her daughter. The message that June got was that, especially if a woman had been molested as a child, 'There's a guarantee that the kids will be. Almost as if I let it happen.'

Even if June had not been a survivor of child sexual abuse, she, as the mother, would still be held responsible for not protecting her daughter from her husband. Somehow, she should have known what was happening. She didn't even suspect Jim.

Well, if you can't leave your kid with their father, who the hell can you leave them with? So a normal mother has to keep the kid tied to her side till the kid's off and married?

What a responsibility to put on mothers.

Along with the housework, the cooking, the shopping. People also say to me, you know, 'Didn't you see it?' See what? Pam had insecurity problems. Sometimes she wouldn't go to Jim when she wasn't feeling good, she went to me.

June found that to some people it wasn't really that much of a problem.

And people were saying I was being too harsh about it, a common thing, a part of growing up. It doesn't have to be. It's got to stop somewhere and I'm going to stop it here anyway. Yeah, we were molested, it's part of life. We talked to people, they were all molested. It's part of life, part of growing up and my Mom came right out and said: 'That happens all the time.'

So all along this was considered normal?

Yeah. OK with me. I would accept it but when it came down to my daughter, no way. And even the police weren't going to do anything.

There was a great deal of anger and conflict in all June's relationships – between her and her sister, between her and her mother and between her and her daughter. Pam blames her mother for making her father go away. June is left to deal with the anger of family and friends as well as that of her daughter.

'I hate you! You made Dad go away.' I just tell her that I didn't tell him to do those bad things and he should have known that they were wrong and no, I'm protecting you. I won't let it happen again. I realize that I'm the only one that she can let her frustrations out on and I'm the closest one, so everything is directed at me.

As with the other interviews, June's interview makes apparent the movement of the focus of anger from the perpetrators to the women in the family. In June's family, anger takes the form of blame, jealousy, resentment and a wish for revenge.

Moreover, June is convinced that Garth also abused Pam and Karen.

A couple days after Jim was arrested, she [Pam] said, 'How
come Uncle Garth isn't?' And she said it was him that was
putting his penis in front of them and asking them to kiss
it, that her Dad only touched her.

June's belief that there is still another man out there likely to be
continuing to abuse Karen has resulted in heated arguments between
June and her sister Maggie.

I finally had it with my sister. She said to me, 'If you had
given your husband what he wanted, he wouldn't have
picked on my daughter.' And I says, 'No way! He got it every
day, twice a day when necessary,' and I says, 'You're not
laying that on me for him being sick.' And she kept it up,
kept it up. She says, 'Your daughter's sicker than mine
because she has to see a psychiatrist three times a week.'
And I says, 'She's not seeing a psychiatrist. That's a diagnostic
programme and it's to help bring her confidence back.'

So push got to shove and I told her about her common-
law [Garth], and I says, 'He's the one threatening the kids
and molesting them.' [Maggie replied] 'Bullshit! You're
just lying because you don't have a man, you're jealous.'
And she married him in September anyway. 'As long as he
keeps buying me things,' she says to my other sister [Alice],
'I'll side with Garth until it can be proven.' And she'll keep
her daughter quiet. So until Pam is confident enough to
speak up, he's out loose, doing what he's doing.

The prevalent myth that incest is caused by women not fulfilling men's
sexual desires has become a weapon here, one used by one sister against
the other. So is the comparison of whose daughter has been more
damaged by the sexual abuse.

June suspects Maggie of having or wanting to have an affair with
Jim.

At one point, when [Alice] and I were still talking, we
thought it was just a ploy by [Maggie] to try [to get my
husband]. She was always most relaxed and what not
around Jim and always saying, 'Let's go to the park.' Pam
and I would go for a nap and the three of them [Jim,
Maggie and Karen] would go to the park. Seeing that I
wasn't going to drop him on my own and she couldn't have
him, he didn't want any permanent thing with her, she had
to settle with Garth. She would always phone for Jim to go

down on his day off. I don't know. Just a whole bunch of things seemed to point at that. That there's no way to get him. A week or two after Jim was charged and Garth was going nuts, I started to question maybe Jim isn't the only one. Because Karen went and jumped into bed with Maggie. She [Maggie] said, 'Fucking drop it. Jim is guilty, he's charged, he's confessed, drop it. Just drop it!' And she constantly [said], 'Drop it.' Just that firmness. She didn't want to know anything. And she said: 'I hope he rots in hell.' The sudden change in her attitude towards him.

She told [Jim] of her sexual relationship with Garth. She never talked to me about it. She had endometriosis and I guess it was kind of painful to have intercourse and what not. She told all this to Jim, but very little of it to me. She's confiding in him more than me. It almost seemed like she wanted him and since she couldn't get him away, been trying for twelve years, neither of us could have him. He was going to be out of the family and that was it.

The question of who was responsible for the sexual abuse of the two young girls became an argument over the attention of a man. June was afraid of her angry feelings and her fantasies of revenge. She spent a great deal of time plotting ways of driving Maggie and Garth crazy. She went to a counsellor to help her get through this obsession with revenge.

I was plotting as to how I could get people's minds to twist and send them off the deep end. Just get them twitching in their chairs like everyone had done to me. Like in little notes. My sister got married and I had thought of sending a note to be put in an assertive way, saying, 'Sorry to learn of your animosity toward me and that it's stronger than our sisterly bond, but time tells all, hope you're very happy in your new life together, love June.' [But instead] I put in the card, 'Love is gentle, Love is kind, Love is caring, sharing.'

So that scared me. It's not me, it's just revenge. I didn't want to continue, 'cause it could prove to be quite dangerous and I don't want to purposely hurt anybody. I got that out of my system and I still send her a birthday card. I sent one to Jim and it says, 'I hope today is just the beginning of another wonderful year for you.' It can throw your mind if you read between the lines, but it's a beautiful card if [you

don't]. It was a bit of spitefulness. And the wedding card
[I sent to Maggie] was along the same line.

Because [Maggie] didn't wreck my marriage, but as soon
as they said, 'It's Jim,' I ended it there. But [Maggie felt] 'May
he rot in hell, drop the whole situation. It's [Jim], he's the
only one [abuser] in the world.' She was just so closed-
minded about the whole thing. She's not helping in the
fight against it, so she's helping to it.

Maggie focuses all of her anger on June's husband, Jim, while exoner-
ating Garth of abusing the girls. This makes June very angry.

June wasn't invited to the wedding in September. Her sister was going
to invite her and let her decide whether or not to come, but Garth
threatened to call off the wedding.

He will still get his [just dessert] and I will have the last laugh.
My sister will end up in an asylum with a nervous breakdown
the way she is. Because she will just not accept it. Now when
they do get Pam talking – and I hate talking about the
situation with Pam around, I refuse to do that in most cases,
or I leave out names and stuff – Karen's Mom continues to
[say], 'Uncle Jim did this, Pam did this, remember? It was
Uncle Jim that did this.' So they won't go after Garth
without some firm ground [that he has been abusing the
girls].

June is quite capable of identifying the feelings she had towards Maggie
and Garth. She wished for justice and also felt alone and jealous of
her sister.

I went as far as I could. I wouldn't accept that being enough
but now I do, bringing it to their attention and what not,
[Family and Children's Services'] attention. And they know
that I've confronted Maggie about Garth. So when they get
charged I'll go up to them [Family and Children's Services]
and say, 'What took you so long?' Or, 'I told you so, you
wouldn't believe me.' There is some jealousy there because
it is your husband, your sister charged your husband. She's
happy with her second husband and you don't have
anybody.

June had documented interactions with Maggie and Garth, doctor's dates,
infections, daycare dates and times when Pam was babysat by Maggie

and Garth. But professionals involved with June also see her wanting Garth charged as revenge.

> My caseworker even said to me, 'If it ever comes about that we charge Garth with molesting Pam, the courts will see it as revenge.' And I said, 'What are you talking about?' 'Well, it would be so many years after.' Oh, I was using some choice words on the phone.

At the time of our interview June had a rather cool relationship with her mother. They had been able to help each other out in very practical ways, although the distrust between the two and the anger was tangible. Her mother lost her job and June got her into a new one and gave her room and board in the townhouse for $10 a day. There were arguments about that.

> 'That's too much, I can't afford it, I got my bills!' 'Give your notice, find a place here, I'm not doing any favours for you, you think I'm getting rich on that?' I says, 'You come home, you sit in a chair. You know, I come home after appointments, I still have to make supper.'
> So if Maggie will do Mom favours or what not then Mom will side with her. She goes and tells Maggie things that I do. I don't care ... I was becoming so defensive when Mom says, 'Martin [a male friend] is calling at night, what's he calling for?' 'Well, what are you saying?' I says, 'Everybody in London has me and Martin sleeping together. Who's been spreading that?' 'I don't know, I don't know.' There's only one person that knows when Martin calls and when Martin comes. Well, I just told them that he came and he called. I says, 'You have no business going and telling everybody what I'm doing.' I guess it wasn't long ago that she commented, 'Well, it [sexual abuse] does happen quite often, all the time.' If people would not let it happen, then it wouldn't be the norm!

June had conflicting feelings about her husband and the future of their relationship at the time of the disclosure and she was concerned about the terms of the divorce.

> Everybody was against me. Jim was charged on the 10th of July. It was that same week I went to see the lawyer for custody and ask for divorce; my mind was just blown. The experiences from my past were coming through and all that.

I just figured it was the only way. And then most people sided with Jim, I was being too hard on him. If it was only that – maybe I am, but I think that's not [it]. It was just the icing on the cake because he would pay more attention to my sister and her little girl.

So he's in [a] correctional institute getting therapy. He'll be getting out February 6th. He's applied for parole at the end of the month, December something. He told me today and I told [Family and Children's Services]. 'Here's the agreement,' [I said]. 'You'd better find a loophole before any of this starts because there's been nothing said about [Jim and Pam] being locked in a room at the Child and Parent Place.'[1] They're supervised visits [now]; that's not in the [divorce settlement].

Family and Children's Services obtained a court order for three months of supervised visits and then three months of unsupervised visits for a couple of hours a week. Then Jim can start getting unsupervised weekends with Pam. How does she feel about that?

He's too scared to try it again. He knows: one wrong move and people are going to be pointing the finger anyway. And he's too immature and that too, I don't know if immature is right for that type of – but no. Just knowing that the next time it'll be worse. And I told [Family and Children's Services], if you can't stop this before it starts, then don't bother interrupting [visits], because you've been warned. You've had fair enough time to deal with it. You're not going to let my daughter start having unsupervised visits with her father and then take them away, take that privilege away. There's no reason why they can't start things rolling. And that way it's not in my hands, because [Family and Children's Services] is doing it.

June is not pleased with her husband's assumption that he will be moving back home, or with the psychiatrist's orders that he cannot. She guards her right to make her own decision about the future of this relationship.

---

1. The Child and Parent Place is an agency that supervises visits between parents and children when a court order prevents them from being together unsupervised.

He [child psychiatrist] says that I cannot get back with Jim. He's telling me what to do. 'You don't tell me that I cannot anything,' I says. 'Time will tell.' He says, 'You cannot, he will do it again.' I says, 'You're biased.' There are some that do it again, but [from] what I've found out from [Family and Children's Services] and different people [there are some that don't]. I says, '[Family and Children's Services] allows the molesters to go back into the family setting. They would rather have father, mother, children relationships in the community.' He [the psychiatrist] can't tell me [what to do]. There are some that repeat, but there are some that don't. They learn their lesson after being caught. And he says, 'Well, I wish you luck.' I don't know, there's something about him, maybe he is a molester himself.

June's husband has kept in contact with June and Pam by phone.

Well, he'll be moping around and he'll phone up and tell me all his sob stories. After I had stored his stuff, then he said something or I said something and he says, 'Oh, I thought I could move back in with you when I get out.' Just assumed that. I says, 'I was doing you a favour by storing your stuff. No need to assume anything. You're not moving back in so fast.' I've been going at everyone else's pace and when they wanted it, when it was convenient for them.

I asked June where she saw herself in, say, another year.

Proving myself. Like I've been so programmed to make everyone else happy. Make sure everyone else is at ease and I totally forgot myself. I didn't know, I'm still not too sure what I want and if somebody asks if I want to go to [a] show [I say,] 'Sure. What would you like to see?' I don't know. I don't know what things interest me. I know game shows don't. My mother's always got them on. She hates MASH and I hate game shows. Seeing's how I have to take Pam up for her bath, my mother wins. It will be a year of looking for me. I have been searching for me and found a bit more; it will be more of a test once Jim gets out. Because he's not grasping a heck of a lot.

June looking for 'me' will mean redefining her relationships with her family and husband.

The second meeting

June's second interview, like the first, centres around her relationships with her ex-husband, her daughter, sisters and, more frequently, herself. June trusts very few people and has had little reason to trust the people in her life, including her ex-husband. His efforts to please her, especially with material things, do not impress June.

> He keeps patting himself on the back because now he's able to manage money. It used to burn holes in his pockets before. Whoopee do. He's more thoughtful. He buys me stuff for Mother's Day and Valentine's and Easter and all the occasions. When we were together, he didn't think of it. Now he's always thinking of us, that he can buy us, I guess. But last year I told him I wasn't his mother. So this year he gives me a gift and he said, 'Don't say what you did last year either.' So I just took the gift and [said] 'Thank you.' Try and buy me, go right ahead. I'll take it but you're not getting nowhere. I deserve some things after all this time …
>
> If it wasn't for me sitting down at the last minute [at Christmas time] and writing a list of things, I guess I would want. Searching through the catalogues. I didn't know what I wanted. And if I didn't write down a few things, I would've got nothing and everything I put on the list was under the tree. Nothing extra. Nothing different. Like, he couldn't put any thought into me, to pick a gift for me, which really hurt. You know we were married for twelve years. Don't you know me? Don't you know what I like by now? You've been so self-centred and I've centred everything around you two [so] that I'm lost in the underbrush.

While Jim was in jail and now that he is out, June has found that a lot of support has been directed at her ex-husband but little support or credit for surviving has been directed towards June and her daughter.

> My brother's wife up north, I haven't heard from her for a while. I wonder if [it's because I] didn't reply to her letter because it was to Mrs Jim … on the envelope and then on the other side there was to Jim, June and Pam. 'How's

everything going?' And then it [was clear] it was a letter to Jim. 'It must be terrible for you in there and you guys are still friends so I just know you'll get back together and that's why I'm writing.' This is a family letter, but it wasn't directed at me, it was directed at him. We had moved. She didn't ask how I was doing, how Pam was doing, how we were settling in, nothing. Just, 'It must be hell.' So I was quite upset with that letter. They're all supporting him. Poor Jim, he's in jail. It must be tough for him. And we've got a piece of cake here.

During Jim's time in jail, June moved to a less expensive townhouse. Without Jim's income, she qualified for a government subsidy to help pay the rent, but the original townhouse was still too expensive.

And Jim is oh, crying about money matters. He's looking for an apartment. The lawyer cost him $100 just to look at these papers for family court, he's paying his Mom room and board, he's got to start paying me support in June. And I says, 'Yeah, we've just been sailing along.' I've managed the other townhouse. [It was subsidized,] but still [it was difficult]. It seemed to be easier than when he was there, when we had a higher income. But [the rent] was $750 plus utilities, and you know nobody's looking at any of the accomplishments I've done.

The original divorce agreement provided insufficient protection for Pam, and Family and Children's Services went to court to extend supervised visitation for another six months. June is in agreement that the divorce decree did not protect Pam sufficiently.

It stated that for three months after incarceration he would have Pam supervised, and after that, liberal access weekends and overnights. I read the divorce agreement but I didn't pick up on it. It was supposed to be gradual. Three months supervised at Child and Parent Place, three months supervised by a mutual friend of ours, and then unsupervised afternoons and then overnights and then weekends. Approximately three months for each. But it does say it goes from supervision to total weekends. So [Family and Children's Services] took us to court and they got six months' supervised visitation extension and Jim is supposed to go to the perpetrators' group run by [Family and

Children's Services] in Milton. He kept saying, 'I've done my time, what more do you want with me?'

Did Jim get any help in prison?

Yeah, he got some, but he needs a lot more. Like he keeps saying, 'Yeah, what I did was wrong but it wasn't that bad. I didn't kill her.' Because he was so down, I guess, the psychiatrists and psychologists – somebody – told him, 'Look it's not the worst thing you could have done in your life.' You know, so they downgraded it. The judge told me that I shouldn't be bothering [Family and Children's Services]. That it should be my responsibility to make sure he doesn't get Pam unsupervised. And maybe, possibly, I supervise them. That's what the courts suggested. And I've blown up at [Family and Children's Services] before for suggesting that. Because neither of them [Jim or Pam] are well enough and they've too far to go ... [Family and Children's Services] will think we're a family [because] the three of us go in the car, wherever. And we're a family automatically in their heads. So to hell with what I want.

June resisted being forced into increased interaction with her ex-husband until Family and Children's Services finally took responsibility for preventing Pam's abuser/father from having unlimited access to her. Because June resisted, it was implied that she was unwilling to keep Pam safe.

I told them, 'I'm not going to do it any more. I'm tired.' I says, 'You don't like it, you do something about it 'cause I'm not gonna [supervise them]. It's going by the divorce agreement and that's that.' Like people have said, you wouldn't [allow unsupervised access to Pam]! I says, 'Probably not,' but I says, 'I'm tired.' You know, I'm not going to be the bully [and deny Pam seeing her father]. It's bad enough I have to take her there and pick her up and, you know, talk to him about her and what not.

How did she make the decision to divorce her husband so early on after the disclosure?

Suddenness. I decided that's the way it had to be, but if there had been no disclosure we would still be together. Because of the situation, I chose; it was the only way to go. I didn't feel, I still don't feel I had any other choice but to get out.

Lumbering idiot, you know. Just waiting for him, keep seeing him all the time when Pam's in bed.

The week I saw the lawyer to draw up the custody and what not, I filed for divorce. There's still a question of whether or not we would get back together, but I do not want the strain [of saying] we are still together and so I just cut all ties and if we get back together it will be my choice. Not just because we're only separated and it's better for Pam. [Without a divorce] I would be too easily coaxed into that, but if you're totally cut off and then get back together, you're more likely to keep a little more caution.

'Cause I knew that in order to find me, I had to be totally free of all ties except Pam. You know, I couldn't get away from that. If I really wanted to I guess I could, eh? But I guess that's not what I really want. I just knew I couldn't [rely on myself] totally, because when you hit a roadblock it's easier to turn back than push your way through. If we were just separated, I'd come to a roadblock and [think] 'I don't have to do this 'cause he'll take me any way I am.' With the divorce, then I have to do this if I'm going to find anybody.

So being free from that helps her?

Yeah, it was just that little security, I guess. Why fight for the moon when you've got something here? So I just knew right from the beginning that in order to get anywhere with myself I would have to tie it off, cut it all loose, and that's what I did.

Other women in June's Mothers' Group have struggled with the same decision about their relationships with their husbands. What do they think?

I've been with lots who are still together and they find it hard because it's just easier to hold on to what you know. And then I've met some that are just new at this and you can hear that they can be easily swayed back to the abuser. But as a lot of people have pointed out to me, I did the extreme. I didn't have to get divorced, you know.

But, I asked, was that the right decision for her? June replied, 'Yeah and to hell with him. He caused the problem.'

June's ex-husband attended counselling and a men's group for offenders at the time he was released. He quit counselling once he was free but continued with the men's group: it was a part of his probation order.

Every so often June mentioned having a strong sense of reality, even though she has had disturbing intrusions like the visions mentioned in the first interview. This sense of reality is a part of evaluating her life and relationships.

It's really hard to say, but the reality in me is very strong. The reality that I am a single mother, I've been abused, my daughter's been abused and we have to deal with that. And me being happy with a man will take time, quite a bit of time. I'm not searching. It will come.

I have some male friends, but I keep them separate from Pam. I could easily get any of them to fulfil a father figure. Make them come over when Pam's awake and what not. No. I need time for me. I fulfil Pam's needs. She probably won't accept a father figure. She would probably make the other person feel quite out of place. And so I meet with them at nights and when Pam's visiting her father, or if I can get my mother to take her. Watch her for me when I go to a dance. Or just sit around and talk.

June still has difficulty helping her daughter control her behaviour. She has learned some behaviour management techniques and Pam continues to see a therapist. June's family has not been very supportive of her efforts.

They notice that Pam's still a spoiled brat. I guess they don't realize that I kind of ignore her for my peace of mind sometimes when she gets uncontrollable. And quite often I say, 'Say so, tell her. You don't like her whining, tell her.' We went to my sister's Easter weekend, the oldest one. We've been there a couple times since she started talking to us again. And I used to use assertiveness on Pam. They were trying to get her to stop her whining and they were ready to give in and I said, 'It's your choice, you can finish your supper, you can do whatever after you've finished eating.' 'Well, can I just eat the bun?' 'That is your supper, when you are finished you can go play.' 'Well I don't like it. I don't like the fat wiener, dinner franks.' So my sister cut it in half and Pam's still balking at it. I [behaved] very calmly, and they were getting perturbed. And she ate it all. [Alice] says,

'I was ready to throw her out the window. I can't stand that whining.' I says, 'I have learned to cope with it.' I get my way, but it's her choice. So [Alice] just says, 'Yeah it does work.' That's why I have to handle just about everything. When she [Pam] wants something and she's whining, then she doesn't get it until the whining stops.

June and Pam's therapist do not agree on ways of helping Pam.

I still don't understand her [Pam], she's into this letting her anger out and calling me names constantly when she doesn't get her own way. I guess it was before I got the tape [on behaviour management] and I was ignoring her and discussed it with her therapist and what not. 'You can't let her do that.' She's got all this anger. She's got to let it out and I let her. 'You still can't let her.' So she [therapist] says, 'Lock her in her room.' You can't do that. She [therapist] says, 'Yes.' And I said, 'The neighbours call the cops because she can hold out longer than I can.' You put a lock on the outside of the room. So I discussed it with quite a few people and none of them agreed with that.

And so I had read through the one [children's] story about the *Berenstien Bear's Bad Habits*[2] where [the little bear] got ten pennies each morning and however many fingernails she chewed that day she had to pay back that many pennies. So Pam gets three nickels a day. One for morning, one for afternoon, one for after supper, and if she calls me a name during any of those periods then she loses that nickel. And she only lost a couple. Now we just do it for something to do and that [money becomes] her allowance. And I did the same thing. I have nickels, three a day, and I've had to pay her a couple of times. I figured if she's got to watch her mouth then so do I.

So I thought maybe I could empty out the storage room and put a lock on the outside of it. But I couldn't see that. Especially [not to use] her bedroom for punishment. And that's where some not too nice things happened and she was constantly coming into bed with me, crawling in during the night. And the therapist is there, 'Why don't you put her back?' Either I don't notice until morning or

---

2. One in a series of popular North American children's stories about a family of bears.

I'm just too tired, can't be bothered with the fight. 'Who is it hurting?' I said. She needs to know I'm there, it makes her feel more secure because we just moved there. She did it for a couple of months. And she [therapist] says, 'What if you have a friend over?' I says, 'Well, I'm not in any position to have a friend over for the total night.' Once she gets more secure then it won't be a problem.

And then she was having bad dreams quite a bit and for a while she was going through those witches under the bed and things in the closet, so I scared them away. Got down and started [looking for them], and they were gone. I had heard [how to do that] somewhere, though. It wasn't my own thing. She kept having bad dreams and I told her it was only her imagination, but I gave her my love doll. You have to see her. I keep telling people about her, nobody gets to see her. Pam won't let go of it. Santa Claus brought me [the doll] for Christmas. So I says, 'Tell you what. You can sleep with my love doll.' I says, 'See all the love she has there? She won't let any bad dreams come.' So she's had very few since letting her sleep with that doll. She's come into my bedroom very seldom.

For herself, June has joined a group for women who were sexually abused as children. She identifies her anger as an important issue arising out of the group.

I'm into my second session of Survivors' Group. I'll probably continue; I'm not sure. I'm getting stuff out of it, but not about my sexual abuse background. It's bringing out different feelings, like they all talk about their fears and, you know, they're afraid of the dark or afraid of this or afraid of that. And I thought and thought and thought. I'm not afraid of anything. The only thing I'm afraid of is myself if I get angry. I'm afraid to get angry because I could kill. But other than that I walk with a kind of air around me of, 'Just try it. Come and get me, try it.' You know? And then there's anger. [I'm] going to a two-part session put on by [a local counselling agency] on anger. Tomorrow night and next Wednesday. I'm not sure what it's supposed to deal with; all I know is I want to know more about anger, 'cause I'm not allowed to express it and I have so much bottled up. It's one extreme to the other. So I know I bite my tongue and keep it in. Eventually I punch a wall or something. I got to be able to tell somebody that pissed me off, but I'm afraid to hurt their feelings.

June's anger has emerged in her dealings with Family and Children's Services and reflects on her history with the agency.

But [the Family and Children's Services worker], every time I talk to her I blow up. And she commented last time, 'How come you get mad at me every time we talk?' I says, 'You're there. It's the agency I'm mad at. You stand for the agency.' And I says, 'You have to prove the agency to me. It's in your hands.' Anyways, all my life I grew up with [Family and Children's Services] around and they didn't do any damn good, [not] a bit of good. I says, 'You took my sisters away for a couple of months and sent them right back to get beat and everything else.' And so I was the protector. The two oldest were taken away and I guess I've seen enough of that when I was protecting all the younger ones and making sure they had everything they needed. They would need shoes, my parents would balk at that and so I'd use my babysitting money and go and buy them shoes and bras.

June talked about her family and the abuse to which she and her siblings were subjected.

I saw them all get thrown around. I don't remember being thrown around or hit, which I know I'm blocking out, I have to be. So I guess I must be blocking it out good. 'Cause I can't see where my father would throw seven kids around, and I'm the third oldest, [and he] never touched me. Most of us have the same perpetrators. My oldest sister said my father abused her for quite a while. I forget how old I was, but she would talk against my Dad and say that's why she got pregnant when she was 13, because she was defying him because he was sexually molesting her.

I didn't believe her because I saw how rotten she was, defiant. But now I'm understanding more. She said she would have nightmares of milking a cow. She was milking a cow and myself and the sister between us two were watching and she'd wake up in a sweat screaming. It finally dawned on her that she was jacking off my father and she said there was a new baby in the house, so that puts me at about 18 months old, when I was hiding in the corners.

It started very early and I keep questioning, why was I hiding in the corners at two? I had two older sisters and they [were] running around. And then when I was five they sent me out west because I wasn't talking. Got out west and they couldn't shut me up. Got back home, I clammed up again. I don't remember out west at all. I remember being taken from the house and out to the train. That should've been exciting. I couldn't remember any of that. It's blocked. That makes me a lot more curious. Other people shrug it off, 'So I don't remember.' But it makes me curious to find out about me and why, 'cause that's not normal, so I'm not normal. Because I was abused I'm not normal. But I just twisted that around and said, 'You're the one that's not normal. You weren't abused.'

June has involved herself in a personal search to find out how she became the person she is and to explore the various feelings that she experiences.

And my counsellor's gonna set up for me to go to group therapy. Just therapy in general. So I guess the Survivors' Group has triggered a lot of different emotions in me that I can't find, or maybe I start to wonder if it's really my emotions. So maybe for now I won't need the Survivors' Group when this other group starts up. [The Survivors' Group] is helping, but I guess somebody with more traumatic experiences of abuse could use my [place].

So would she like to do more with the emotional part?

That is what is bothering me the most. I knew that I was abused and that my abuse caused me to have the characteristics that I have now, but I thought dealing with that or getting into that would even trigger more memories that I could understand why I am the way I am. But it's really not working that way. I am coming [along], but it's hard.

Every step along the way, whether in discovering more about herself or in learning to help her daughter, June has met resistance. Who were her biggest critics?

My ex-brother-in-law, my sister's old husband, who is Jim's ex-boss, and then some people I work with. They all knew the old me anyway and I guess they liked me doing everything, bending over backwards, and so they're always questioning why I'm trying something new.

This included criticism of June's taking an assertiveness training course.

They said: 'You just tell people what you want and you don't have to spend money and take an assertiveness course.' They were trying to get me out of it and I couldn't do it on my own. I needed the courses. And this anger one, I'm not sure what it is, what I'm going to find in it, but it sparks an interest. You know, you get angry but it's not the right way or the right time, or I withhold a lot and [get]: 'Oh, I've seen you mad, don't give me that bullshit, who are you trying to fool?' But they don't totally know me.

And my ex-brother-in-law says, 'Better watch it, watch it. You may not be able to handle it [the Survivors' Group].' I haven't figured out quite what he's trying to do, except get me to quit, so I'm still vulnerable. Or maybe he did something to me 20 years ago when he first got together with my sister and doesn't want me to remember. And he's there, trying to scare me to not go for the group, to the Survivors' Group. But I'm stubborn. When I've made a decision to do something and somebody tries to talk me out of it, that makes me more determined. And my mother said, 'What do you need another group for?' She says, 'You're doing OK.' [I say,] ''Cause I want to do better.' And she just kinda [goes]: 'Huh.' So yeah, I got a lot of people saying that. About the only ones that are saying, 'Good, go for it' are the therapists and [Family and Children's Services], the authority figures. But anyone lower than that ...

June has noticed through her participation in the Mothers' Group that identifying needs and making decisions, especially about relationships with husbands, is very difficult. Once again, keeping responsibility for the abuse focused on the perpetrator is difficult.

Well, in listening to others I've found that it's really hard for them to decide what they need, what their needs are, and a lot of them for a long time cannot decide whether they want their husband or they don't want their husband.

If the kids are older then they tend to blame the child for coming on to the husband, their male. I guess I did that too, but not with Pam because I saw how Karen was all over men and so I know what I saw that one Christmas. And then with her coming on to Pam, I guess I still blame her, blame Karen, for a lot of it.

So I guess I'm guilty in that area too. I didn't blame my daughter but I blamed the other little girl, other victim. Because they were all picking on her [Pam] and [me], physically on her and mentally on me. My sister and Jim were both saying, 'Drop it, you're imagining things, there's nothing going on.' You know, my sister had no right to say that unless she knows of something.

June and her daughter remain on their own for the time being. June is very clear about taking her time in considering any relationship and that her relationship with herself and her daughter is of primary importance.

6 Discussion

Anger

This book would not be complete without some mention of anger. My own experience of asking about the lives of women who are mothers of children sexually abused by their fathers/stepfathers has sometimes been one of receiving anger. It was not uncommon to be asked by others, including other professionals, what I was writing about. That I was trying to relate the actual experience of mothers of sexually abused children was an insufficient response for a surprising number of people. From my own peers there were occasionally angry responses, questions of 'Well, did they know their children were being abused?', implications of presumed failure as parents, and several offers of literature that would 'enlighten' me as to the responsibility of parents (= MOTHERS).

I became increasingly reluctant to share this project with others and I could feel myself shrink inside when that familiar question was raised. In this way I imagine I came to experience a very small measure of the anger frequently levelled at mothers and perhaps, to a greater extent, the pressure to silence the voices of women, especially those of mothers. One of the greatest fears I had as I began writing about these women was that instead of being viewed as the experience of four women, the writing, by its very subject, would result in more anger being directed at them. Our society is constructed in such a way as to make women, especially mothers, the repositories of our society's anger. Both men and women come to blame mothers and many professionals come to do the same thing.

Responsibility for the sexual abuse of female children is not focused for long on the male perpetrators: fathers and husbands. This was most apparent in the first interviews. Instead, I found the anger that one might expect to be directed at the men who sexually abused the daughters of the women interviewed was almost exclusively directed at women. Anger could be seen to filter down past the perpetrators and land on mothers, daughters and sisters. This anger took the form of blaming, interpersonal conflict and depression. The women in this work may or may not have identified themselves as being angry or as receiving anger from others. These are my interpretations.

Laura

Laura briefly expressed her anger with her husband but is quite torn between her continued love for her husband and the reality of the abuse. Instead of keeping her anger focused on her husband, she redirects it to Tom's parents and their competence as parents. They have reared a man capable of sexually abusing her daughter and have failed to provide him with an appropriate role model for husband and father. This failure of others in some part absolves Laura's husband of the responsibility of the abuse and makes him deserving of understanding and pity instead of anger. There is no frame for directing anger at men; rather, there is the fulfilment of women's skills in being empathetic, understanding and meeting their men's emotional needs.

Some of Laura's anger can also be seen to surface as she talks about her daughter. Laura was quick to respond to her daughter's needs after the disclosure and continues to do so when the opportunity arises. The anger I am referring to takes the form of resentment and some jealousy: resentment at being manipulated, forced to choose between daughter and husband; jealousy of her daughter's youth and opportunity for healing and starting her adult life. Neither of these things is in any way a comment on Laura's 'goodness' or 'badness' as a parent. In many ways Laura epitomizes what in our society would be considered the 'good mother'. These are simply examples of what forms of anger are legitimate for women and who may legitimately be the focus of anger.

Beth

Beth exonerates her husband's abusive behaviour by attributing it to a sort of illness, like alcoholism. She tries to be understanding and a medical reference assists her in finding an empathetic response. Beth at one time blamed her daughter for the abuse, but now her anger has turned inwards and she has taken on responsibility for what happened to her children and the damage done.

Fay

Fay's anger found expression in two significant ways. First, it was expressed in a response to oppression. It was internalized as depression which, despite medication, continued to remind her of her powerlessness and the impossibility of finding a 'right' response. Second, it was clearly directed at the systems that promised to protect her daughter but failed to do so. As Fay talked about her efforts at moving the courts, police, politicians and other professionals to help protect her daughter, her voice briefly reflected that anger and its energy. Then her voice returned to its original monotone.

June

June's anger and rage find voice in a variety of ways, some of which have probably become more vivid in the wake of her own history of abuse. Shortly after the disclosure, June experienced visions in which she saw herself stabbing her husband or she saw her daughter's death. These were frightening visions for her, as was her experience of trying to push her own head under water. Her revenge fantasies towards her husband, brother-in-law and sister seem to me an expression of anger which is private and also powerless: the only way for June to gain some control over a situation in which she was powerless and not believed. June feared this part of her as 'not her'.

Another expression of anger is the fighting, arguing and distancing between June and her mother and between June and her sisters. Conflict remains between the women in the family, taking the form of seemingly trivial arguments over men. For example, June was accused by her sister of wanting Garth charged just because she was jealous that she didn't have a man. There is conflict with June's mother over the mother's 'gossip' about June's private life, about childcare and rent. Far from being trivial, the anger expressed in these areas is in legitimate areas for women's concern. The conflict continuously circulates between the women, unresolved and far away from the abuse by the husband, and possibly by the brother-in-law, of two little girls. Arguing over the latter would be too dangerous to maintain for long. June also endures the anger of both family and friends, who feel she is making too much of a 'normal' occurrence and that she is being too hard on her husband.

Naomi Scheman (1980) has explored anger, its discovery and how what counts as anger can be changed. Much of what I have identified as anger in the women's experiences may be a budding feeling that cannot be directly expressed in a society which denies women's anger and forbids focusing this emotion on the male perpetrators of abuse. To some extent what I have called 'anger' is a political redescription of the women's experience and may not be identified as anger by them.

> The bestowing or the withholding of a name can be personally and politically explosive. To see that some state of affairs counts as oppression or exploitation, or that one's own feelings count as dissatisfaction or anger is already to change the nature of that situation or those feelings. (Scheman, 1980, p. 181)

By the time of the second interviews Beth, Laura and June are clear in their focus and they hold their husbands responsible for the abuse. Laura both still loves her husband *and* is angry with him. She tolerates the tension in this situation. Beth also has mixed feelings towards her husband. As Laura explained in her second interview, her Mothers' Group allows the women involved to share their anger towards their spouses, including rage and revenge fantasies, without negative feedback. Other women are angry too; and the expression of revenge fantasies is a welcome relief and is experienced as liberating. Recovery from the disorientation after the initial disclosure of the sexual abuse of their daughters made the women more focused in their anger. It also made them more able to feel anger at the same time as other emotions, such as love for a spouse.

Division of responsibility

At some point in our interviews, three of the women reflected on their relationships with their husbands and the sort of reparations the men were, or were not, attempting to make. What I saw in these reflections was, first, how reparations through the legal system in the form of time served or time spent in counselling was assumed by the men, at least initially, to be payment in total. There seemed to be a simple, linear relationship understood between the crime and the punishment. Second, as discussed above, anger could not be focused for long on the perpetrator; the effort by men to participate in counselling or to remain attached to the family was appreciated by the women, but not expected. The women, consistent with their position in society, were unquestionably wedded to their responsibilities of maintaining the family and relationships even after the form of the family had changed. I saw this as a given for the women, optional for the men. When it came to responsibilities after disclosure, there were many prescriptions for women – appointments to keep for counselling, courts, Family and Children's Services, involvement in parenting and other 'self-development' courses – but very few for the men. And third, despite their hopes for a renewed relationship with their husbands, both Laura and Beth voiced concerns that their husbands might be capable of abusing other children and were already taking on the responsibility of becoming future watchers of their grandchildren.

Laura's husband, like June's husband, initially had difficulty accepting that he would not be allowed immediately back into the house. Laura:

> He is very hopeful [to move back home]. Last Thursday he was sitting here and I guess he had [had] a session with J [his therapist] and he was saying how far he had to come. We talked about the fact that he knew when he left the house that this was not a short-term project. That's why at first he was in a rooming house and J also helped [him] to understand that he was punishing himself, 'cause it was a real dive affair. His clothes were getting mouldy and everything else. So anyway, he has sublet this apartment and it's a decent apartment on 8th Street and there's a swimming pool. Because he realizes that it is long term and he also realizes that he will not come back into our lives unless Susan allows it.

Tom was looking for quick answers to solve the problems following his daughter's disclosure of the sexual abuse.

> He keeps trying to repair things, keeps trying to problem-solve, and he hasn't gone far enough. He's had one or two sessions with J. But he, for the first time, admitted through many, many tears how wrong he was about some of the things and how he has got to learn to change his thinking and his reactions and his reasons. And he wished to heaven he had done this years before. Unfortunately, one of the

reasons he did it is because my husband can be quite the con artist. He's very charming, suave; he's a salesman. He said a lot of the reason he didn't go for help was the fact that he feared that with the new legislation [mandatory reporting of child sexual abuse], whoever he went to had no other thing to resort to than to have him charged, to report it because she was under 16.

Any effort Tom has made to attend counselling or to attempt change has been supported by Laura. Laura sees her continued support of Tom and the maintenance of their relationship as essential to the continuance of Tom's effort to change. Her role as woman, as mother, as wife, continues even with the family's changed form.

There was a lot of times I would think, 'Hey, just let it slide, it's not important, keep the peace.' So that has changed. We have talked about that quite frankly and he has said, 'There's no way I will let you take back the old Tom.' So as I say, he kept saying, 'I have so far to come.' He said, 'I cannot believe in looking at my life that I could be such a bloody lowlife,' but he said, 'I was and I'm not happy with that and if I don't change now, I'm never going to change.' And he said, 'If I don't change, there's no way I want to live. Because,' he said, 'I can't accept that in another person and I will not accept it in myself.' So, you know, I think he will try, but I think he will try only as long as I am on his side.

He would not continue if he didn't feel Laura supported him?

No, I then think he would drop out of counselling. I think he would try to rebuild his life with somebody else. Just shut out that part of it.

So, I suggested, a lot of him, a lot of the change that maybe he's trying to make now is invested in the thought that the family will be the family again? Laura replied, 'That's right. I'm sure of it. Having known my husband for 28 years.'

Beth's husband, Conrad, also participated in counselling after the disclosure. Her decision to separate while she took some time to get her own life back together was a surprise to him. From his point of view, he was doing his part by going to counselling and he expected that the end result would be a continued relationship with Beth.

And when he went into counselling last year, he was working at it. I knew he was working at it, he really was.

But it just seemed to me like it was going to take forever and I didn't have forever to wait. You know, I just got to that point where I wasn't sure and so he really resented the fact when we had to split up this time because he couldn't understand why I was doing it now and not then.

Despite being separated from Conrad and often angry, Beth has constantly supported his attempts to get help and to change through AA and individual counselling. By their own choice, both Conrad and Tom continued in individual counselling well after the second interviews. Taking responsibility for sexually abusing their daughters and the horrible consequences on the lives of these girls was a long time coming. For both men, minimization of the abuse and the time it would take to heal was eventually replaced by a longer-term commitment to change through therapy.

June's husband, however, was unable to move past his severe minimization of the abuse. He was in prison when June and I met to talk about her experience. At that time she was still storing his belongings and selling some items, as he needed money to pay monthly loan obligations. He would like her to do more.

And he's giving me the sob story, when he gets out February 6th then come the 15th he has to come up with $300 support. 'Yeah,' I says, 'you'll have to start back-payments too.' I managed, found my way through. $750 rent plus utilities. I've found different programmes that help out, so you [Jim] can't make me feel guilty. I've done without. And when I move, I'll put his stuff in storage and give him the bill.

Like Laura's husband, June's husband assumed that once he had fulfilled his obligation to the courts, he would be able to resume his life with June and their daughter, Pam. He could not understand what more she could possibly want from him. After all, he had done his time in prison. Jim also continued to minimize the importance of his sexual abuse of their daughter well after his release from prison. In his own words, 'What I did was wrong but it wasn't that bad. I didn't kill her.' June has recognized Jim's minimization and inability to accept responsibility for the assault of their daughter and continues to keep her daughter safe from possibly being re-victimized by her father.

Many and complex demands are made of mothers after the sexual abuse of their daughters by fathers or stepfathers. Realistically, mothers presently and historically have been responsible for the well-being of

everyone in the family. Demands on men in terms of making reparation
for the damage of sexual abuse of children are not high. In essence then,
women have no way of not taking responsibility.

Loss of self and recovery

Women's role in our society has been to maintain the family. In
fact, women are expected to meet the needs of men and of
children before their own needs.[1] More recent psychological
theories of women's development have made the point that
women develop differently to men, with greater emphasis on
continuity and connection with others rather than on separation
and autonomy.[2] Jean Baker Miller (1976) has stated that 'women's
sense of self becomes very much organized around being able to
make and then to maintain affiliation and relationships' (p. 83).
Women's sense of self or self-definition is threatened by the possibility of severed relationships. When a woman's self-worth
comes solely from keeping the family together and she is deemed
responsible by society for keeping the family together, what is the
impact of disclosure of sexual abuse? How does she deal with such
a disclosure?

Although each woman in this book acted differently in response
to her daughter's disclosure of having been sexually abused, there
were similarities in their subjective experiences. Each woman
described a sense of confusion, of an internal disorganization as
well as external. Their lives became suddenly disorganized, with
phrases such as 'life in tatters' and 'life in shreds' being used to
describe the experience. Beth saw that everything was falling
apart and wondered out loud 'how to keep it together?' Three of
the women verbalized the loss felt at not being a family, or the
need to be a family again. The disintegration of the family and
loss of roles and relationships within the family was disorienting
for all of the women. One of Beth's proudest moments was being
able to say that she and her children were a family once more.

Laura also spoke of her loss in terms of her changed relationship with her husband. She said, 'I've come to the realization that
what I am doing is grieving my marriage. It's like a death, except
you don't have people around to support you. It's [even] like your

---

1.   Miller, 1976.
2.   Gilligan, 1982.

husband is dead, but nobody knows it. So you have to grieve by
yourself.'

Recovery for at least two of the women involved working
through the feelings of being lost or confused in order to find out
who they were. Both Beth and Fay clearly expressed their need
to know themselves better. All of the women were attempting to
start identifying and meeting their own needs.

What has impressed me about all four women I interviewed is
their survival after what must have been an experience in direct
contradiction with their socialization and psychological development as women. There seems to be no way for them to have
made sense of the events following disclosure. The maintenance
of the relationships within the family changes as the family,
without exception, falls apart. This becomes a disorganizing
experience from which a different sense of self is eventually constructed and seen as 'recovery'.

The process of recovery was also different for each woman. It
was apparent in the second interviews that this recovery process
was well under way. The disorientation of the initial time of
disclosure had cleared and effects such as depression had lifted.
Each woman had recovered her ability to make decisions and
establish goals and direction in her life. A great deal of introspection
was apparent and was probably encouraged by involvement in
various therapies, but there was also an exploration of the outside
world, including the prevalence of violence and abuse. Moreover,
several women felt the need to explore their relationship with what
they saw as 'God' and spirituality. What appeared to be least
resolved by the second interview for three of the women was their
relationship with the abuser. Responsibility for the abuse had long
ago been established and maintained, but the mixed feelings
they have towards their husbands is especially difficult for Laura
and Beth. They have developed an ability to be simultaneously
angry at and fond of their husbands, and they are able to express
that.

That the confusion does lift, the pain does become less, decisions
do become easier to make, relationships can heal and the process
of recovery can be a healing and beneficial one is a message of
hope from the women interviewed here to other mothers of
sexually abused children. It does get better, but for each woman
this process of recovery, and discovery, took time and was still
apparent one year after the first interview.

Services

Responsibility for the cohesion of the family in our society has, as mentioned previously, historically fallen to women. Mothers work routinely towards meeting the needs of men and children. At the time of disclosure of sexual abuse the rules suddenly change. The mother finds herself in the position of having to make a choice that will inevitably result in the dissolution of the family. This choice is diametrically opposed to her socialization as a female in a patriarchal society which has prepared her to take care of men and to maintain the relationships of family. Clearly, any choice that she will make will be unsatisfactory.

Each woman interviewed commented on the feeling of confusion following her daughter's disclosure or discovery of the abuse. The sudden impending loss of relationships and concomitant loss of self in those relationships placed enormous stress on the women. Added to this was the mother's continued responsibilities with the service providers, making sure that appointments were kept with Family and Children's Services, counsellors, the court system and others. Three women interviewed were unable to continue working due to the stress of the days, weeks and months following disclosure. All suffered such reactions as sleeplessness, depression, loss of appetite, increased use of alcohol and lack of concentration.

From the time of disclosure to well after the second interviews the women were involved in a variety of resources or agencies. Although services such as support groups for mothers of sexually abused children and some individual counsellors and workers were regarded positively, the women all related treatment by service providers that was less than adequate. The parenting abilities of the mother seem immediately suspect when sexual abuse is disclosed. In Laura's story I saw the role of her daughter's counsellor as quite effectively usurping Laura's role as mother. The psychiatrist who treated June's daughter attempted to have her taken away from June when she began reacting to the stress of her daughter's abuse and its effect in triggering memories of her own abuse. Women were sent to parenting courses and assertiveness training – sending a clear message about responsibility for children and women's role in the protection of children. I would not dispute the possible benefits of the skills learned in such courses; rather, I would call attention to the underlying message regarding the role of mothers and our society's efforts to retrain them after they have 'failed' to prevent husbands and fathers from sexually abusing their daughters.

Finding resources when needed was often difficult. Those which were used varied for each woman in kind as well as in usefulness. The only resource which each woman used consistently and which was unanimously regarded as useful was the Mothers' Group.

The Mothers' Group was the only constant resource over the year for all of the women interviewed. The group introduced the women to peers: other women who had experienced similar trauma and feelings, and a variety of reactions to the disclosure of the sexual abuse of their children. The kind of sharing that was allowed in the group would probably have been discouraged in other helping settings or would not have been shared because of the individual nature of the help. Laura had this to say about her experience of the group:

> Well, through this whole year I think the greatest thing, the greatest help, has been Mothers' Group. There you have the support of other women, you help other women. I have talked about issues that I never even knew I had feelings on and boy have I had feelings on them! I have said things in Mothers' that I wouldn't say in a confessional. And yet, you know, it's funny. I can remember standing there one time and saying how I could kill my husband and every single mother in the room said, 'Oh you've experienced the same thing that we have.' 'I wasn't going to stab him with a knife, I was going to poison him.' 'You know, if he was standing here in front of me today I could just keep kicking him until he couldn't take any more.' Every single one of the mothers felt the same thing.

Another advantage that many peer group settings offer, including the Mothers' Group, is the sense of not being alone. Says Laura,

> Well it was such a one-ness. I'm not alone. This feeling is not unique. Like, you could express your anger and nobody was going to jump down your throat for it. The best thing of all is the fact that, as I say, I talked about things that I had buried so deep for so long, and I think most of the mothers are doing the same thing. It's a great group, you just simply go and whoever has the greatest problem that day is the first to speak, and mostly it's bad but occasion-

ally it's good where somebody is really starting to heal and then they'll say, 'I had a fantastic week and I just want to share it with you.' You know, this is what happened and that type of thing. But usually it's the bad things that are happening in your life right now, how your emotions are, how depressed you are and the fact that you may be a super-clean mom [but right now you] couldn't care if [you] ever cleaned this house again. I wouldn't pick up a vacuum cleaner for a month and with a dog around, you're talking disaster. Wouldn't dust the furniture. The only thing I did was cook and load and unload the dishwasher.

So you'd go in and say to somebody, 'Did you do your laundry yet?' And they'd say, 'Have you vacuumed yet?' And it was done with a smile and with understanding because, as I say, a lot of them had been through the same thing.

The group also reflected the experiences of women at different stages in their own recovery or healing processes and allowed the women to be both supported and a support to other women. Becoming a support for other women was an empowering experience for some of those interviewed. Beth shared her experience of providing phone support to another woman.

I like the telephone bit, I really do. I think that's instant number one. Through the group, I speak to a lady a couple of times a week that hasn't been able to get out to the meetings and she's never been, so [the facilitator of our Mothers' Group] sort of lined her up with me. She's an older lady. But I find talking to her on the phone gives me a sense of comfort, knowing that I can still help somebody. I mean, I don't want to be active right now because I tend to get too involved. But it also gives me a chance to give back a little bit and I know how I felt.

She's going to start going [to the group] now that she can, but I've probably been doing this for, I don't know, three months. So she says she feels like she knows me and we've discussed it and it's something you can talk to somebody over the phone. Although I've never met her. I think I'm going to meet her tomorrow night. She's supposed to be there. I think the self-help services like that where you do have a phone line, an open phone line, like a buddy system is really good in the programmes now. I don't know

how much they do that in the self-help groups. I know
there's a phone system and that everybody gets numbers,
but I don't think everybody uses it. And I think it's really
important that rather than you get a list of names or
numbers to call that a buddy system is really promoted.

That you do have a one on one even if the counsellors
match up two people that are similar. And say to each one
in the beginning, 'Could you possibly give a call every
week or every couple of weeks?' If they want to, that's
fine. After the initial talking they'll decide themselves
whether they're comfortable in that situation. I think that
kind of feedback is really, really good so they can go back
and tell their counsellor that this one [match] isn't working,
that I really don't have a lot in common [with her] or that
I find her very distant or whatever.

But I like the idea of [the] telephone. It just means that
there is somebody there, and there's someone that cares.
The funniest part that I find when I call this lady (she's never
called me as of yet, and I've called her, I don't know,
between one and two [times a] week usually, because again
I don't believe in bugging and pushing; I think you have
to set a reasonable time), she's said, 'Beth, I'm so glad you
called, I was just thinking about you today. It's amazing
how you always hit on, when I need you right now.' And
I think that happens a lot of times in a lot of situations.

Many women found that the family itself was eventually inundated
with services and that it was important, after the confusion began to
subside, to be discerning about which services to keep and which to let
go. Laura's family had quite an itinerary of counselling services.

As I say Tuesday night we have couple's [therapy] every
second week, Wednesday afternoon I go for private counselling, Wednesday night I would have Mothers' [Group].
And that was just my counselling. Tuesday, at lunch, a
mother from out of town would call me. And my husband
was going to Offenders' [Group] on Wednesday, Thursday
morning was his counselling with [his therapist] and
Thursday night was Alanon. So we were spending so much
time away from other things we wanted to do, and the kids
– you have to get choosy. If this isn't working, then give
it up, and I don't care if you're paying for it or getting it
for free. I don't think I would have made it without Mothers'

simply because when the abuse was disclosed, as a mother you need something immediate where you can vent your pain, your anger, your fear. And until [a group facilitator] got me into Mothers', I had no place. I called every agency, and that was in May, and the waiting lists, at the earliest, [ran to] September.

Fay had the same advice for women.

I learned, I guess, for one thing: don't take everything. There are things [where] you can take the advice, but there's also some stuff you can just throw away that you don't need. And eventually you'll learn how to make that decision. In the beginning I think you just take everybody's advice. Eventually you can say, 'I didn't need that,' but at the time you thought you did.

In addition to there being few services available specifically to mothers of sexually abused children, it is often difficult for women to access the services that do exist.

[When you are] calling around for help, you're calling blind. And I found it very difficult because each [agency] has an intake officer [or secretary]. You're talking to a secretary at the other end of the line, you don't know what she looks like but she's asking you very personal questions and she wants your name and address and phone number and why are you calling? [She says,] 'Your daughter was sexually abused. Well, I'll certainly give this information to the intake officer.' I don't know her from Adam! I don't know if she's the cleaning lady answering the phone because it's lunchtime.

Each woman interviewed contributed a message of what might have been helpful to her. An underlying concern was that there should be someone available who wouldn't add to the blame that the women felt around them. All women felt that a service to meet the needs of mothers would have to be immediate. Laura suggested there should be a service that would be more intensive than the weekly Mothers' Group and could be accessed immediately, especially in the first few weeks after disclosure. She would have liked a one-to-one kind of service that a woman could call at any time of day that wouldn't necessarily have to be structured. Beth suggested a phone service like an answering service. June liked the Mothers' Group, and was also thankful for the services of the Child

and Parent Place which allowed her daughter to visit her husband in
safety once access was allowed him.

Another need identified by Laura was for a place where the women
could begin to express the myriad feelings they were experiencing,
including those which might have seemed unacceptable.

> If we had more areas like Mothers'. That's all that we need
> as far as expressing, getting rid of our anger, our hurt, this
> type of thing. I think counsellors [are OK], if they could
> spend more time trying to stress the positive.

More support- and action-oriented?

> Mothers' even does that to some degree, through the
> leaders. And oftentimes a lot of the older Moms support
> the new ones because they've been through it and worked
> at using first-hand experience as far as the courts are
> concerned – Family and Children's Services and things
> like that.

*The involvement of Family and Children's Services was without
exception a traumatic experience for the women interviewed. For Beth
this involvement contributed greatly to her confusion and disorientation.*

> I just think that as the system sits right now, that it's just
> so difficult for everybody. Especially when kids are taken
> [from the] home and things like that. Obviously this is very
> traumatic for everyone and I would never want to see
> anybody in a situation where it was unhealthy and they
> weren't protected. But I just think that sometimes it's as
> much trauma tearing a child away from a situation, as
> they do in many cases, as it would be just to have someone
> sitting down with them and talking with them, everybody
> talking together, or they had some [sorting out of the
> situation] beforehand. And I really think a kids' helpline[3]
> in that situation is a really good idea.

*Disappointment with Family and Children's Services did not seem to
stem from a wish that disclosure hadn't taken place or that children
didn't need protection. On the contrary, many of the women discussed*

---

3.   Childline in UK: (NSPCC). Freephone 0800 800 500. Kid's Help
     Phone in Canada: 1 800 668 6868.

ways of protecting children and, in the stories of Fay and June, several obstacles to keeping their children safe could be identified. The difficulty the women had with the services had more to do with the recovery required from the trauma of involvement and sudden breaking apart of the family.

> I know there are times when that has to happen. It just seems to me like that's what happens. Like the police come – with the [Family and Children's Services] somebody's put here, he's taken away. It's just all too much for everybody to even comprehend it at times. Much less make any sense. Like I don't think there's ever an absolute solution there, obviously. Every situation is different.

Fay felt that the moment a child confided sexual abuse to an adult, the system swung into operation and there was no turning back, no possibility of finding an alternative route to dealing with the problem. Her greatest need was to find an alternative that would allow the family to stay together and prevent the kind of quick decision that she was forced to make. She suggested there should be an alternative that would see a family worker immediately placed in the home to provide supervision of the family and allow the decision-making process to slow down, and not to rest solely on the shoulders of the mother.

A serious concern of the women interviewed involves the perception by workers, agencies and family members that mothers do not require support. Beth felt this minimizing attitude from her husband among others.

> I've always said the offenders get all the attention they could ever want and more. The victims for the most part do as well and, aside from this, I don't think the mothers get a heck of a lot – or the other partner, not necessarily just mothers. But I think they sort of get left out, and not just in the role of you not knowing about this or being left out of the family situation. I don't think the husband or the offenders think that this affects us at all. I mean, my husband is the worst one of them. I don't think he has any idea of why this would ever have affected me in a million years.

Beth also talked about being blamed initially by her daughters for lack of protection, although Beth did not know about the abuse. Neither her husband nor her children could understand how she might be affected by the knowledge that her husband had been sexually abusing her children.

Like, 'What's this got to do with you?' Excuse me, but I now don't have a marriage, you know. And I think too the kids tend to [feel the same]. I'm lucky, but I know in the beginning my kids would basically [say], 'What's this got to do with you, you didn't do anything? You didn't do anything to help even if you didn't know. What did it do to you? I mean, we're the ones that got hurt here.' So I don't think anybody thinks that we, as mothers, have any feelings, I guess. That we have any emotions in this, that we are as much traumatized by this as the other two parties. It's pure and simple trauma.

There's no two ways about it. Our lives are destroyed as much as anybody else's, damn it. And I don't think, lots of times, that anybody gives us that. If I was talking to the police right now, they wouldn't [understand] and I don't think that any of the other agencies out there [would either], unless you're doing one-on-one counselling and you're really lucky enough to [get] somebody who really understands. They're still minimizing the fact that there's any real great trauma in our part in this and [they think] that we should be supporting the other two parties, but the support's gotta come this way too. This is my story, this is what it is. It doesn't change. That's the way life is, you know. You don't make this up as you go along. It just happens.

Fay expressed thankfulness for almost every service that she came in contact with over the previous year and a half. Each agency or helping person had some significance for her.

Thanks. It's just tear-jerking. Good or bad, they've all taught me something. I wouldn't have known a good one from a bad one if I hadn't gone through it. Even the decisions I let Parents Are People Too[4] make. That was a bad experience for me, but it was also helpful because I learned from it. I don't know. It's just been a great experience and I thank everybody that helped me.

June reiterated the opinion of the other three women that there should be someone to talk to immediately. Waiting lists for counselling were prohibitively long and a source of frustration and distress for these mothers.

---

4. A Canadian peer-support group for parents experiencing difficulties with their children, especially teenagers.

*Their daughters and husbands received some sort of attention imme-
diately. The mothers, already under a great deal of stress, took care of
getting other family members to their appointments but waited to have
their own needs for support met. Service provision came to reflect what
typically plays out in families: the needs of men and children come first,
with the underlying message that good mothers have no needs but to
meet the needs of others. Once women entered therapy, however, they
were encouraged, sometimes for the first time, to begin meeting some
of their own needs. The rules changed once more.*

*My involvement with Laura, Fay, Beth and June has had implica-
tions for my own work with women. What impressed me most was the
importance of their recovery and the place of anger within that process.
Immediately following disclosure was a time of great stress and confusion
for the women. No matter what action was taken in response to the
disclosure, each woman described feelings of anger, which were
sometimes directed towards the daughter in the form of blame. Following
the women as they recovered allowed me to see the movement of that
anger over time away from the daughters. That such a change takes
place has important implications for all workers who work with
daughters, mothers and families. It means that supporting individuals and families through this process is very important, as is watching
that mothers and daughters are not routinely and systemically dis-
connected from one another. The process itself takes time and needs to
be respected. There is a felt need to slow everything down and lessen
the trauma. Decision-making becomes very difficult after disclosure and
the consequences are often serious. Clearly, it would be ill advised to
make assumptions about women and children following disclosure, or
to minimize their pain.*

*What would allow mothers to have the kind of support that both
their daughters and the perpetrators have? Peer support groups with facil-
itation, such as the Mothers' Group, provided the greatest support for
women over time. As well as the message that help is needed immediately, I would add that support and counselling should be separated.
In my opinion, mothers need someone who is going to be present just
for them, who is not going to be invested in anyone else in the family.
Laura's sense of loss and pain are clear in the following passage from
her first interview, when she described the way services were offered to
other family members but were not available in the same way to her.*

My daughter was taken immediately. My husband was
seen by [a counsellor] immediately. What has my husband
lost? His family, OK. And he did it, he lost it because of his

own actions. But he hasn't lost the financial security, that part of it. My daughter has lost a family voluntarily, she has lost her father whom she has hated anyway, but had to keep it private. So in one respect there's relief for her. Although she has to go through the emotions of guilt and what have you. She now at least can open up about what has been happening to her and say, 'I don't want it any more and I don't like you for doing it.' So she has the option of whether she wants to go public or not, but it satisfies her own needs. Whereas you're there in the middle and all you can do is react. You know and yet you've not had a doggone thing to do with it. I think that's the most maddening part of it, the fact that your whole life is altered and yet nobody ever consulted you, nobody ever asked you. And yet you're the one who has lost the most. I've lost a daughter, I've lost a husband, I've lost my entire way of life, and I'm trying to cope and I've got nobody. And I think I'm fortunate.

Epilogue

It has been two years since I first interviewed the four women for this project. Their lives and those of their families have changed substantially over that time and for most have come to some resolution. I have kept in touch periodically with Laura, Beth, Fay and June, during the writing of this book, and at this point can give the reader an idea of where they are at now.

Laura's daughter, Susan, moved back home two months after our second interview and she has decided to pursue a nursing career, like her mother. Laura's husband and daughter increased their interaction with one another as well as discussions about the abuse and the effects it has had on Susan's life. Laura's husband continues individual counselling as well as couple counselling with Laura. He has recently moved back into the family home. Laura is pleased with the atmosphere in the house but is also cautious. As she says, 'We may not make it, but we'll see.'

Beth's stepdaughter, Jayne, initiated contact with Beth two weeks after she received Beth's letter and they were able to work it through. Beth was able to take her grandkids on holiday and feels that her relationship with her stepdaughter has actually improved. Conrad increased contact with Beth after that and, in the last few months, Beth and Conrad have begun dating again. Beth is not optimistic about their future as a couple. Conrad continues with his counselling.

After a series of brief relationships, which included one with Marcia's abuser, Fay moved to the outskirts of a rural community with a new male friend and her daughter Marcia. Alicia stayed in the city with her boyfriend. Fay has recently gone back to finish high school. Marcia has had difficulty finding either a school or a work setting that she can maintain and, for now, is staying at home. She and her mother continue to have a very stormy relationship. Marcia recently disclosed that she was sexually abused by an uncle several years ago. Fay is assisting Marcia in her wish to press charges and will be supporting her through the court system.

June continues to live in her townhouse with her daughter Pam. She is content, for the moment, to meet her needs for an adult relationship by dating and seeing men when her daughter is not present. She intends to continue group therapy, including working on issues related to having been physically and sexually abused herself as a child.

Appendix
Sexual Assault Services

Compiled by Alex Fenner

Alphabetical by country

AUSTRALIA

Australian Capital Territory

Incest Centre
Canberra
Tel: (06) 249 6070

Social Services

Northern Regional Office
Tel: (06) 207 1069

Southern Regional Office
Tel: (06) 207 1466

New South Wales

Dympna House
Haberfield
Tel: (02) 797 6733

Social Services

Child Protection and
Family Crisis
Tel: (24 Hours) 008 066
777

Northern Territory

Alice Springs Sexual
Assault Referral Centre
Tel: (089) 515 880

Social Services

Child and Family
Protection Service

Alice Springs
Tel: (089) 515 170

Darwin
Tel: (089) 893 939

Katherine
Tel: (089) 738 600

Nhulunbuy
Tel: (089) 872 366

Rural (Aboriginal)
Tel: (089) 228 474

Tennant Creek
Tel: (089) 624 334

Queensland

Social Services

Crisis Care
Tel: (24 Hours) (07) 365
9999

Family Services
Tel: (07) 224 8045

South Australia

Social Services

Adelaide District Office
Tel: (08) 304 0120

Information Line
Tel: (08) 226 7000

Tasmania

Social Services

Child Protection Unit
Tel: (002) 332 921

Victoria

Social Services

Ballarat
Tel: (054) 345 555

Eastern Metro
Tel: (03) 248 7248

Geelong
Tel: (052) 264 540

Gippsland
Tel: (051) 762 500

Grampion
Tel: (053) 332 944

Hume Highway
Tel: (057) 602 266

Northern Metro
Tel: (03) 412 5333

Southern Metro
Tel: (03) 706 8143

Western Metro
Tel: (03) 275 7000

Western Australia

Social Services

Crisis Care Line
Tel: (24 Hours) 008 199
008

Families Helpline
Tel: 008 643 000

CANADA

Alberta

Calgary Communities
Against Sexual Abuse
Calgary
Tel: (403) 237 5888

Sexual Assault Center of
Edmonton
Tel: (403) 423 4121

British Columbia

Sexual Abuse Support
Service
Parksville
Tel: (604) 248 2093

Vancouver Rape Relief
and Women's Shelter
Tel: (604) 872 8212

Victoria Women's Sexual
Assault Centre
Tel: (604) 383 3232

Manitoba

Sexual Assault Crisis
Program
Winnipeg
Tel: (204) 786 8631

New Brunswick

Fredericton Rape Crisis
Center
Tel: (506) 454 0437

Newfoundland

St John's Rape Crisis and
Information Center
Tel: (709) 726 1411

Northwest Territories

Alison McAter House
Yellowknife
Tel: Crisis Line (403) 873
8257

Nova Scotia

Avalon Center
Halifax
Tel: (902) 425 0122

Ontario

Assaulted Women's
Helpline
Toronto
Tel: (24 Hours) (416) 863
0511

Ottawa Rape Crisis
Center
Tel: (613) 729 8889

Sexual Assault Center
London
Tel: (519) 438 2272

Quebec

Sexual Assault Center
Montreal
Tel: (514) 934 4504

Saskatchewan

Regina Sexual Assault
Line
Tel: (306) 352 0434

Saskatoon Sexual Assault
and Information Center
Tel: (306) 244 2224

Yukon

Kaushee's Place,
Woman's Transition
Home
Whitehorse
Tel: (403) 668 5733

IRELAND

Cork Rape Crisis
Helpline: (021) 968 086

Dublin Rape Crisis
Helpline: (01) 661 4911

Galway Rape Crisis
Helpline: Freephone
1850 355 355

NEW ZEALAND

Auckland

Help Foundation
Tel: (24 Hours) (09) 623
1700

South Auckland Help
Foundation
Tel: (09) 277 9324

Christchurch

Rape Crisis Incest
Survivors Group
Tel: Crisis Line (03) 364
7324

Wellington

Sexual Abuse Help
Foundation
Tel: Crisis Line (04) 801
8178

Wellington Rape Crisis
Tel: (04) 385 9880

SOUTH AFRICA

National Childline
Tel: Freephone 0800
123 321

Resources Aimed at the
Prevention of Child
Abuse and Neglect
(RAPCAN)
Cape Town
Tel: (021) 685 6011

People Opposed to
Women Abuse (POWA)
Johannesburg
Tel: (011) 642 4346

UK

National

NSPCC. 24 Hour
Helpline
Tel: Freephone 0800
800500

Youth Access
Tel: (0116) 255 8763

Avon

NSPCC Mothers' Group
Bristol
Tel: (0117) 966 4283

Bedfordshire

Bedfordshire Sexual
Abuse Helpline
Luton
Helpline: (01582) 33592

Berkshire

Reading Rape Crisis Line
Helpline: (01734)
575577

Buckinghamshire

Milton Keynes Rape
Crisis Centre
Helpline: (01908)
691969

Cambridgeshire

Choices
Cambridge
Helpline: (01223) 467
897

Cheshire

Ellesmere Port Family
and Child Therapy
Service
Tel: (0151) 356 1009

Cleveland

Cleveland Rape and
Sexual Abuse Coun-
selling Service
Middlesbrough
Helpline: (01642)
225787

Cornwall

Cornwall Rape and
Sexual Abuse Helpline
Camborne
Helpline: (01209)
713407

Cumbria

Mothers of Abused
Children
Silloth
Helpline: (016973)
31432

Derbyshire

S.A.I.L. (Sexual Abuse
and Incest Line)
Chesterfield
Tel: (01246) 556 114

Devon

Checkpoint
Torquay
Helpline: (01803) 200
100

Dorset

East Dorset Rape Crisis
Poole
Helpline: (01202) 547
445

R.A.I.L. (Rape Abuse and
Incest Line)
Bournemouth
Helpline: (01202) 311
115

Essex

CASAC Mothers' Group
Harlow
Helpline: (01279) 444
487

Gloucestershire

Survivors of Child Abuse
Gloucester
Tel: (01452) 309 026

Greater Manchester

Family Contact Line
Altrincham
Tel: (0161) 941401

Manchester Rape Crisis
Helpline: (0161) 834
8784

Hampshire

Off The Record
Havant
Helpline: (01705)
474724

Portsmouth Area Rape
Crisis Service
North End
Helpline: (01705)
669511

Southampton Rape
Crisis Line
Helpline: (01703)
701213

Hereford and Worcester

Women's Aid
Hereford
Tel: (01432) 356146

Hertfordshire

Herts Area Rape Crisis
Centre
Ware
Helpline: (01707)
276512

Humberside

Childwatch
Hull
Tel: (01482) 25552

Kent

Kent Child Protection
Team
Chatham
Helpline: (01634) 815300

Leicestershire

Leicester Rape Crisis
Helpline: (0116) 270
6990

Lincolnshire

Ask
Lincoln
Tel: (01522) 514244

London

London Rape Crisis Line
Tel: (0171) 837 1600

East

Inner City Centre
Tel: (0171) 738 0195

North

Consultants to Adult
Survivors of Abuse
(CASA)
Tel: (0181) 345 6688

In Support of Sexually
Abused Children (ISO-
SAC)
Tel: (0171) 284 2125

South

Maya Project
Tel: (0171) 731 4907

Rape and Sexual Abuse
Support Centre
Helpline: (0181) 689
8181

West

Hounslow Survivors of
Sexual Abuse
Helpline: (0181) 890
4732

Merseyside

The Salisbury Centre
Mothers' Group
Wirral
Tel: (0151) 639 0761

Wirral Rape Crisis Coun-
selling Service
Birkenhead
Tel: (0151) 666 1392

Norfolk

Norwich Rape Crisis Line
Helpline: (01603)
667687

Northamptonshire

Northamptonshire Rape
and Incest Crisis Centre
Northampton
Helpline: (01604)
250721

Nottinghamshire

Nottingham Rape Crisis
Centre
Helpline: (0115) 941
0440

Oxfordshire

Oxford Sexual Abuse and
Rape Crisis Centre
Helpline: (01865)
726295

Shropshire

Shropshire Rape Crisis
Centre
Telford
Helpline: (01952)
248444

Staffordshire

North Staffordshire Rape
and Crisis Centre
Stoke on Trent
Helpline: (01782)
204177

Suffolk

Suffolk Rape Crisis
Ipswich
Helpline: (01473) 715333

Surrey

Kingston Women's
Centre
Kingston upon Thames
Tel: (0181) 541 1964

Sussex

Brighton Rape Crisis
Helpline: (01273)
203773

NSPCC East Sussex Child
Protection Team
St Leonards on Sea
Tel: (01424) 428833

Tyne and Wear

The Kite Mothers' Group
Sunderland
Tel: (0191) 567 4801

Tyneside Rape Crisis
Centre
Newcastle upon Tyne
Helpline: (0191) 232
9858

West Midlands

Child Protection Team
Mothers' Group
Dudley
Tel: (01384) 456738

Victim Support Rape
Crisis Counselling
Service
Wolverhampton
Helpline: (01902) 27223

Yorkshire

Bradford Rape Crisis
Helpline: (01274)
308270

Doncaster Rape Crisis
Centre
Helpline: (0132) 360421

Leeds Rape Crisis Centre
Helpline: (0113) 244
1323

York Rape Crisis
Helpline: (01904)
610917

Northern Ireland

Belfast Rape and Sexual
Abuse Centre
Helpline: (01232)
249696

Nexus Institute
Belfast
Tel: (01232) 326803

Scotland
Dundee Rape Crisis
Helpline: (01382) 201291

Hamilton Women's Aid
Helpline: (01698)
891498

Mothers of Sexually
Abused Children
Edinburgh
Helpline: (0131) 226
5515

Rape and Abuse Line
Highlands and Islands
Helpline: (01349) 865316

Women's Support
Project
Glasgow
Tel: (0141) 556 5669
(Qwrty 0141 556 5205)

Wales
Cardiff Women's Aid
Tel: (01222) 390874

Swansea Incest Helpline
Helpline: (01792)
648805

*Other Useful
Organisations*

British Association for
the Prevention and
Sway of Child Abuse and
Neglect (BAPSCAN)
10 Priory Street
York
North Yorkshire YO1 1EZ
Tel: (01904) 613 605

Standing Committee on
Sexual Abuse
of Children (SCOSAC)
73 St Charles Square
London W10 6EJ
Tel: (0181) 960 6376

The Child Abuse Studies
Unit
University of London
Ladbroke House
62–66 Highbury Grove
London N5 2AD
Tel: (0171) 607 2789

USA

Alabama

Council Against
Rape/Lighthouse
Montgomery
Hotline: (334) 286 5987

Alaska

Standing Together
Against Rape
Anchorage
Hotline: 1800 478 8999

Women in Crisis-
Counseling and
Assistance, Inc.
Fairbanks
Tel: (907) 452 7273

Arizona

Center Against Sexual
Abuse
Phoenix
Hotline: (602) 241 9010

Arkansas

Arkansas Coalition
Against Violence to
Women and Children
Little Rock
Hotline: 1800 332 4443

West Arkansas
Counseling and
Guidance Center
Fort Smith
Tel: (501) 452 6650

California

California State
Coalition of Rape Crisis
Centers, c/o LACAAW
Los Angeles
Hotline: (213) 626 3393

Colorado

Colorado Coalition
Against Sexual Assault
(CCASA)
Denver
Tel: (303) 861 7033

Sexual Assault Team
Grand Junction
Tel: (303) 243 0190

Connecticut

Connecticut Sexual
Assault Crisis Services,
Inc. (CONNSACS)
East Hartford
Tel: (203) 282 9881

Sexual Assault Crisis
Service, YWCA
Hartford
Tel: (203) 522 6666

Delaware

Rape Crisis Center of
Wilmington
Tel: (302) 761 9100

District of Columbia

D.C. Rape Crisis Center
Washington
Hotline: (202) 333 7273

Florida

The Adult and
Adolescent Sexual
Assault Program
Jacksonville
Tel: (904) 355 7273

The Florida Council of
Sexual Abuse Services
Inc.
Jacksonville
Hotline: 1800 226 6667

Georgia

Georgia Network to End
Sexual Assault, c/o Rape
Response, Inc.
Gainesville
Tel: (404) 503 7273

Rape Crisis Center
Atlanta
Tel: (404) 616 4861

Hawaii

Hawaii State Coalition
Against Sexual Assault
Honolulu
Hotline: (808) 524 7273

Idaho

Idaho Coalition Against
Sexual and Domestic
Violence
Boise
Tel: (208) 384 0419

Rape Crisis Alliance
Boise
Tel: (208) 345 7273

Illinois

Illinois Coalition Against
Sexual Assault (ICASA)
Springfield
Tel: (217) 753 4117

Women's Services, Loop
YWCA
Chicago
Hotline: (312) 372 4105

Indiana

Indiana Coalition
Against Sexual Assault
(INCASA)
Indianapolis
Tel: (317) 568 4001

Prevention of Child
Abuse, Indiana Chapter
Indianapolis
Tel: (317) 624 9282

Sex Offence Services
South Bend
Hotline: (219) 289 4357

Iowa

Iowa Coalition Against
Sexual Assault (Iowa
CASA)
Des Moines
Tel: (515) 242 5096

Sexual Assault Interven-
tion Program, YWCA
Cedar Rapids
Tel: (319) 363 5490

Kansas

Kansas Coalition Against
Sexual and Domestic
Violence (KCSDV)
Topeka
Tel: (913) 232 9784

Kentucky

Rape Victims Services /
OASIS
Owensboro
Hotline: 1800 226 7273

Louisiana

Louisiana Foundation
Against Sexual Assault
(LAFASA)
Independence
Tel: (504) 878 3849

YWCA Rape Crisis
Program
New Orleans
Tel: (504) 483 8888

Maine

Maine Coalition Against
Rape
Augusta
Tel: (207) 759 9985

Maryland

The Sexual Abuse
Treatment Centre
Baltimore
Hotline: (410) 728 7282

Massachusetts

Rape Crisis Centre of
Central Massachusetts
Worcester
Hotline: 1800 870 5905

Rape Crisis Program
New Bedford
Hotline: (508) 999 6636

Michigan

Everywoman's
Place–Crisis Center
Muskegon
Hotline: (616) 722 3333

Sexual Assault Informa-
tion Network of
Michigan
Midland
Tel: (517) 832 0662

Minnesota

Minnesota Coalition
Against Sexual Assault
(MCASA)
Minneapolis
Tel: (612) 872 7734

Mississippi

Gulf Coast Women's
Center
Biloxi
Hotline: (601) 435 1968

Mississippi Coalition
Against Sexual Assault
Jackson
Tel: (601) 960 7470

Missouri

Metropolitan Organisa-
tion to Counter Sexual
Assault (MOCSA)
Kansas City
Tel: (816) 931 4527

Montana

Violence Free Crisis Line
Kalispell
Tel: (406) 752 7273

Nebraska

Nebraska Domestic
Violence Sexual Assault
Coalition
Lincoln
Tel: (402) 476 6256

Nevada

Community Action
Against Rape
Las Vegas
Tel: (702) 385 2153

Crisis Coalition Center
Reno
Tel: (702) 323 4533

New Hampshire

Helpline
Concord
Hotline: 1800 852 388

New Hampshire
Coalition Against
Domestic and Sexual
Violence
Concord
Tel: (603) 224 8893

New Jersey

New Jersey Coalition
Against Sexual Assault
(NJCASA)
New Brunswick
Tel: (908) 846 3586

New Mexico

New Mexico Coalition of
Sexual Assault Programs,
Inc.
Albuquerque
Tel: (505) 883 8020

New York

New York State
Coalition Against Sexual
Assault
Albany
Tel: (518) 434 1580

Rape Intervention
Program
New York
Tel: (212) 523 4728

North Carolina

North Carolina
Coalition Against Sexual
Assault (NCCASA)
Lumberton
Tel: (910) 739 6278

North Dakota

NDCAWS-Coalition
Against Sexual Assault in
ND
Bismark
Hotline: 1800 472 2911

Rape and Abuse Crisis
Center
Fargo
Hotline: 1800 627 3675

Ohio

Ohio Coalition on
Sexual Assault (OCOSA)
Columbus
Hotline: (614) 268 3322

Women Helping
Women, Inc.
Cincinnati
Hotline: (513) 381 5610

Oklahoma

Oklahoma Coalition
Against Domestic
Violence and Sexual
Assault
Oklahoma City
Hotline: 1800 522 9054

Women's Resource
Center
Norman
Tel: (405) 360 0590

Oregon

Center Against Rape and
Domestic Violence
Corvallis
Tel: (503) 754 0110

Oregon Coalition Against
Domestic and Sexual
Violence (OCADSV)
Portland
Tel: (503) 223 7411

Portland Women's Crisis
Line
Hotline: (503) 235 5333

Pennsylvania

Pennsylvania Coalition
Against Rape (PCAR)
Harrisburg
Hotline: 1800 692 7445

Pittsburgh Action Against
Rape
Tel: (412) 765 2731

Rhode Island

Rhode Island Rape Crisis
Center
Providence
Tel: (401) 421 4100

South Carolina

People Against Rape
Charleston
Tel: (803) 722 7273

South Carolina Coalition
Against Domestic
Violence and Sexual
Assault
Columbia
Tel: (803) 254 3699

South Dakota

Aberdeen Area Rape Task
Force
Aberdeen
Tel: (605) 226 1212

South Dakota Coalition
Against Domestic
Violence/Sexual Assault
Agency Hill
Tel: (605) 698 4129

Women's Circle Crisis
Line
Sisseton
Hotline: 1800 898 9927

Tennessee

Tennessee Coalition
Against Sexual Assault
Nashville
Hotline: (615) 256 8526

Women's Resource and
Rape Assistance Program
Jackson
Tel: (901) 664 9727

Texas

Rape Crisis and Child
Sexual Abuse Center
Dallas
Tel: (214) 653 8740

Texas Association
Against Sexual Assault
(TAASA)
Austin
Tel: (512) 445 1049

Utah

YWCA / Women's Crisis
Center
Ogden
Tel: (801) 392 7273

Vermont

Vermont Network
Against Domestic
Violence and Sexual
Assault
Montpelier
Tel: (802) 223 1302

Women's Crisis Center
Brattleboro
Tel: (802) 254 6954

Virginia

Virginians Aligned
Against Sexual Assault
(VAASA)
Ivy
Tel: (804) 979 9002

Women's Resource
Center of the New River
Valley
Radford
Tel: (703) 639 1123

Washington

Washington Coalition of
Sexual Assault Programs
(WCSAP)
Olympia
Tel: (206) 754 7583

West Virginia

Sexual Assault Services of
Family Services of
Kanawha Valley
Charleston
Tel: (304) 340 3676

West Virginia
Foundation for Rape
Information and Services
Fairmont
Tel: (304) 366 8126

Wisconsin

Dane County Rape Crisis
Center
Madison
Tel: (608) 251 7273

Wisconsin Coalition
Against Sexual Assault
(WCASA)
Madison
Tel: (608) 257 1516

Wyoming

Self Help Center
Casper
Hotline: (307) 235 2814

Wyoming Coalition
Against Domestic
Violence and Sexual
Assault
Casper
Hotline: 1800 990 3877

References

Bogdan, R. and Taylor, S. (1975). *Introduction to Qualitative Research Methods: A Phenomenological Approach to the Social Sciences*. New York: Wiley.

Butler, S. (1978, 1985). *Conspiracy of Silence: The Trauma of Incest*. San Francisco, California: Volcano Press.

Campbell, B. (1988). *Unofficial Secrets: Child Sexual Abuse – The Cleveland Case*. London: Virago.

Caplan, P. (1985). *The Myth of Women's Masochism*. New York: E.P. Dutton.

Caplan, P. and Hall-McCorquodale, I. (1983). 'Mother-blaming in major clinical journals.' *American Journal of Orthopsychiatry* 55: 345–52.

Driver, E. and Droisen, A. (1989). *Child Sexual Abuse: Feminist Perspectives*. London: Macmillan.

Finkelhor, D. (1979). *Sexually Victimised Children*. New York: Free Press.

Gilligan, C. (1982), *In a Different Voice: Psychological Theory and Women's Development*. Cambridge, Mass.: Harvard University Press.

Hagan, T. (1986). 'Interviewing the downtrodden'. In P. Ashworth and A. Giorgi (eds), *Qualitative Research in Psychology* (pp. 332–60). Pittsburgh: Duquesne University Press.

Herman, J. (1981). *Father–Daughter Incest*. Cambridge, Mass.: Harvard University Press.

Herman, J. and Hirschman, L. (1981). 'Incest between fathers and daughters'. *Women and Mental Health* (pp. 497–505). New York: Basic Books.

Hooper, C. (1992). *Mothers Surviving Child Sexual Abuse*. London: Routledge.

James, K. and MacKinnon, L. (1990). 'The "incestuous family" revisited: a critical analysis of family therapy myths'. *Journal of Marital and Family Therapy* 16 (1), 71–88.

Kelly, L., Regan, L. and Burton, S. (1991). *An Exploratary Study of the Prevalence of Sexual Abuse in a sample of 1244 16–21 year olds*. London: Final report to the Economic and Social Research Council.

Koch, K. and Jarvis, C. (1987). 'Symbiotic mother–daughter relationships in incest families'. *Social Casework: The Journal of Contemporary Social Work*, 68 (2), 94–102.

MacLeod, M. and Saraga, E. (1988). 'Challenging the orthodoxy: towards a feminist theory and practice'. *Feminist Review*, 28, 16–55.

Michell, G. (1988). 'The reproduction of narcissism'. *Women & Therapy*, 7 (4), 35–49.

Miller, J.B. (1976). *Toward a New Psychology of Women*. Boston, Mass.: Beacon Press.

O'Hare, J. and Taylor, K. (1983). 'The reality of incest'. *Women & Therapy*, 2 (2/3), 215–29.

Renvoize, J. (1982). *Incest: A Family Pattern*. London: Routledge & Kegan Paul.

Rossiter, A. (1986). *In Private: An Inquiry into the Construction of Women's Experience of Early Motherhood* (pp. 28–39). Toronto, Women's Press.

Scheman, N. (1980). 'Anger and the politics of naming'. In S. McConnell-Ginet, R. Borker and N. Furman (eds), *Women and Language in Literature and Society* (pp. 174–87). New York: Praeger.

Sgroi, S. (1982). *Handbook of Clinical Intervention in Child Sexual Abuse*. Toronto: Lexington.

Smith, D. (1987). *The everyday world as problematic: A Feminist Method*. Boston, Mass.: Northeastern University Press.

Walkerdine, V. and Lucey, H. (1989). *Democracy in the Kitchen: Regulating Mothers and Socialising Daughters*. London: Virago.